D0827950

Self-
Affirmation

SELF-AFFIRMATION

THE LIFE-CHANGING FORCE OF A CHRISTIAN SELF-IMAGE

GUY GREENFIELD

BAKER BOOK HOUSE
Grand Rapids, Michigan 49516

Copyright 1988 by
Baker Book House Company

ISBN: 0-8010-3820-0

Printed in the United States of America

Scripture quotations not otherwise identified are from the *Holy Bible, New International Version.* Copyright © 1973, 1978, 1984 International Bible Society. Used by permission of Zondervan Bible Publishers.

To

Paige,
Nelson,
and
Todd

Whose self-images their mother and I initially helped to shape
And God is continuing to re-shape in the image of his Son

Contents

Preface

> Two men looked out
> From prison bars;
> One saw the mud,
> The other saw the stars.

What was the difference between these two men? Vision! Internal perception. Self-imagery. The way you see yourself is the way you will see everything and everyone around you. Good vision will set you free to become what God intended you to be. Poor vision will destroy the divine intention within you.

> The one who saw the mud
> Will be like the spring peach blossom
> In an early frost, nipped in the bud.

> The one who saw the stars
> Will forever be set free
> From life's prison bars.

"Visionetics" is the study of the way humans perceive themselves and the way that self-vision affects their behavior. Visionetics is an attempt to explain why some folks are happy and others are sad, why some succeed and others fail, why some love and others hate, why some win and others lose, why some feel good and others feel bad about themselves and life in general.

I have written this book out of several years of observation, reflection, and experience with people. This is not intended to be a technical study in scientific, research-oriented psychology or sociology. It is actually a summary of theological and biblical reflection regarding the way people think, feel, and act. My ultimate goal is to direct the reader toward change and growth in light of God's revelation of himself in Jesus Christ.

It is the nonprofessional lay person both in and out of the church whom I have had in mind as I have written about the self-image. After having plowed through the professional psychological and sociological literature, as well as the relevant theological works on Christian anthropology, and realizing that few writers ever attempt to bring these various disciplines together for the lay person in language that is understandable to common folk, I decided to make my own attempt to explain why people do what they do and to offer a method for change to those who seek a positive, more fulfilling self-image.

The Bible says, "Where there is no vision, the people perish" (Prov. 29:18, KJV). It is also true that where there is poor vision of self, God, and reality, people will fall short of God's purpose for their lives. It is Jesus Christ who offers us the perfect vision of God, self, and life. In him we see the Father and the Father's plan for us as persons and as his people. It is Jesus Christ who also makes possible a positive self-image for each of us, and this new self-image in Christ has great power for changing the direction and character of one's life.

I wish to acknowledge the kind assistance of the administration and trustees of Southwestern Baptist Theological Seminary for making possible the generous sabbatical leave during which time this book was written. I also want to thank the Concord-Kiowa Baptist Association in western Oklahoma for providing my wife and me their furnished missionary apartment and office in Cordell, where this book was written during the winter and spring of 1987. Director of Missions H. Alton Webb graciously sought to meet our every need.

Gratitude is also expressed to Southwestern Oklahoma State

University for offering the use of their library resources as a Scholar-in-Residence during the spring semester of 1987. In addition, I am grateful to the Education Commission of the Southern Baptist Convention and to the T. B. Maston Scholarship Foundation for their generous financial assistance for carrying out this project.

My heartfelt thanks go to the First Baptist Church of Cordell, Oklahoma, who encouraged my writing while I preached to them on Sundays as their Interim-Pastor from December of 1986 through May of 1987. And to Carole, my wife of thirty-five years, goes my undying appreciation for encouraging me to complete this book and for her input of ideas, opinions, and insights, which are scattered throughout its pages. This is as much her book as it is mine. Truly, she is "a wife of noble character. . . . She is worth far more [to me] than rubies" (Prov. 31:10).

Guy Greenfield
Fort Worth, Texas

1

Take a Good Look at Yourself

This book is about you. It will show you why you behave the way you do most of the time. This book is not only an attempt to explain your behavior but also to reveal a plan for changing it for the better. This book is about your self-image, that is, the way you see yourself, your inner vision. It is a study of "visionetics," or self-imaging. Its goal is to guide the reader to learn the art of Christian self-affirmation.

Your self-image holds the key to why you act the way you do. What you see (regarding your "self") is what you do. If you want to change your behavior, then you have to change your self-image.

Let's illustrate this with the example of a twenty-four-year-old white, working-class, Texas-born-and-reared fellow I will call Bob Wilson. (All names in illustrations in this book have been changed to protect the individuals' privacy.) Bob grew up on a farm where he and his father and mother and older brother worked hard to make a living. His father was very demanding and his mother very critical. Their home did not have a happy atmosphere. His older brother, Jim, was his parents' favorite. To them, Bob could never

do anything right. Any expressed humor in the family tended to be
put-downs, usually at Bob's expense.

In his early formative years, Bob heard thousands of messages
from these significant others in his life that could be summarized
as follows: "You are not good enough; you can't do anything right;
you are not competent; you'll never make it; you will never know
success." The bottom line was: "Bob, you are a loser." In time he
believed it.

Bob accepted these "reflected appraisals" of himself and gradually began to see himself as a "loser." The deadly thing about
this was that he felt compelled to prove with his behavior that this
was true. His academic record at school, his work on the farm, his
relationships with his peers, his performance in school sports, as
well as his activity at church, "proved" that Bob was indeed a
"loser."

Upon graduation from high school, Bob tried to make a go of it
in college, but he never made it through his first year. He was failing too many courses. The next few years saw him average about
three job changes a year. He married at age twenty-three, but he
was divorced two years later. What better way to prove you are a
loser than to lose your marriage! To further confirm Bob's negative self-image, he spent a lot of time in chronic depression.
Thoughts regarding suicide, the ultimate confirmation of the
loser status, finally brought Bob for counseling.

Did you notice that I said that Bob had to *prove* that he was a
loser? One way we maintain our "sanity" is to prove to ourselves
and others that our self-image is correct. The vision we have of
ourselves is a sort of script we follow in life's drama. We play out
the role the script calls for. Therefore, our behavior confirms that
our self-perception is correct. This self-imaging determines our
behavior. What Bob Wilson saw in himself was what Bob did in
his actions. He proved that he is a loser.

What is meant by "self-image"? It is the kind of person you see
when you look at or think about yourself. This vision of the self is
closely connected with certain feelings you have about yourself.
In a sense, this is who you are. Regardless of its source or origin,
this self-definition, or self-perception, is who you are. Consequently, what you see is what you are. This vision or perception
may be distorted, twisted, and out-of-focus, but it is reality as far
as you are concerned. Others, for the moment, may see you differ-

ently, but that matters little, if at all. What matters is *your* vision, not theirs.

Working with people over the years has convinced me that the self-image is at the heart of why people do what they do. But more than that, I have concluded that what you see in yourself, the self-vision you carry around inside yourself, determines how you feel about yourself, which in turn determines the degree of your satisfaction with life and the way you treat others. That is to say, the way you treat yourself is the way you will treat other people. Therefore, if you want to treat others well, you need to learn how to be good to yourself. Or, as psychiatrist Hugh Missildine says, learn how to be a good parent to yourself.

It seems to me that Jesus' words about loving one another ought somehow to include loving one's self. And they do! After all, didn't he say something about loving your neighbor as yourself? Those words in Matthew 22:39 speak to the significance of what this book is all about. As you learn to love yourself, so you will be able to learn to love other people. What you do with your own self is the key to what you will do with other selves.

The Self

What is meant by the "self"? Briefly, we generally mean one's total personality, all that one is. But that includes a lot of different dimensions, so there could be a lot of parts to the self. We could therefore speak of several different expressions of the self.

Some have divided one's self-concept into three aspects: (1) cognitive, (2) affective, and (3) behavioral.

Cognitive refers to the self's knowing, reasoning, and thinking. This would include both awareness and judgment. When the self gathers information, knowledge, and facts, and then analyzes and classifies those bits and pieces of data, it is exercising its cognitive ability. The human is a rational being.

Affective refers to the self's capacity to feel the full range of human emotions. Feelings of love and hate, fear and trust, joy and sorrow, anxiety and tranquility, are common emotions that all of us experience almost daily. In the arena of interpersonal relationships, the affective aspect of the self is probably the least understood and the most neglected. Quickly think back over your educational experience and you will probably have to admit, as I

16

have, that the schools you attended taught very little, if anything, substantive about human emotions. And yet this is the area I have had the most trouble with in getting along with other people as well as myself.

Behavioral refers to the self's ability to engage in a variety of actions. This would also include the volitional or decision-making ability of the self. We all choose moment by moment to do certain things. Actually, we are most immediately known for what we do. You can't always see what persons think or feel, but you can observe their actions. The behavioral dimension also includes the intentional facet of the self's actions. The law generally recognizes this. For example, to differentiate between murder, manslaughter, killing in self-defense, and accidental killing, the law addresses the matter of intent. We often ask, "What was that person's motive in doing that?" Intent and motive are important aspects of behavior.

Behavior also relates to ethics, in the sense that actions can be classified as either moral or immoral when measured against some moral standard. A large body of literature has been published dealing with ethical decision making. The way we make decisions determines the nature, direction, and consequences of our behavior. For evangelical Christians, the use of the Bible in ethical decision making is a popular subject on many college and seminary campuses.

In summary, the self is all that you are, the way you think, feel, and behave. The self has a unique identity and character and expresses itself in its motives and decisions. There are no two selves exactly alike. You bear a name, but this is only a surface label or classification. Your self has been the product of a specific culture and environment, but these are only the "clothes" worn by the self. To be sure, these are powerful and shaping influences, but culture, environment, and life experiences provide only the raw material by which the self chooses to come into being as a unique personality. I am who I am because of what was given to me (family influence, status and position in society, culture, environment, and life experiences) *plus* how I responded to what was given to me.

Evangelical Christians would add the blessings and intervention of the God revealed in Jesus Christ as major and determinative factors in who the self becomes, especially following the conversion experience that involves repentance and faith. This could be illustrated by the experience of the English Puritan Richard Baxter who, upon visiting the inmates of an English prison, said, "But for the grace of God, there go I."

Perception

Taking a good look at yourself requires that you be able to see well. Perception is a tricky thing. We sometimes see things that aren't there, and at other times we somehow miss what is actually there. Obviously, I am referring to seeing your inner self and not some material objects in your line of physical vision. I am discussing psychological, interior, and subjective vision. What do you see when you look at your inner self?

There are two kinds of perception: *authentic* and *imagined*. The first would conform to objective, measurable facts with which most rational people would agree. The second is a matter of definition (more on this later, when we explain "definition of the situation"). But, for now, imagined perception can be just as effective and influential as authentic vision. What we "image" is just as real as "reality" if we truly believe it to be so.

Our college theater department once produced a stage play in which one of the most beautiful girls on campus was chosen to play the role of a backwoods hag. Carolyn had a terrific positive self-image, perceiving herself to be a "beautiful" young woman. Yet the theater department's makeup artist in one hour converted that gorgeous female into an unsightly wretch, fit for the part the dramatist envisioned when he wrote the play. But the external change did not alter the girl's self-image. When the makeup came off, Carolyn continued to perceive herself to be "beautiful." Back in the dorm, on a date, or in class, she looked the part that she perceived herself to be. Her appearance in the play was only external and temporary. On stage she was "ugly," but on campus she was "beautiful." Perception made the difference.

The next year our college saw just the opposite situation take place. The theater department chose a rather ordinary "plain Jane" to play the part of a "beautiful" woman. Marsha had never caught the eye of any male on campus and was never asked out for a date. Her usual appearance simply showed no taste. Most of the time in class she looked like she had just gotten out of bed and never checked herself in the mirror. But the stage makeup artist turned this drab creature into a ravishing beauty. The male actors had a hard time concentrating on their lines when the new Marsha walked on stage.

Yet, inside, Marsha still saw herself as "ugly." Back on campus in the dorm or in class, she returned to her old drab self in both looks and behavior. Her perception had not really been altered by the makeup artistry. The director of the play could change Marsha's looks and actions in only a temporary and superficial way. Her imagined perception overruled potential reality. An authentically beautiful person was buried by an imagined perception. What Marsha saw was what Marsha did.

Moreover, perception actually works on three levels. First, there is your true self-image, how you really see yourself, what you think you are. Second, there is your presented image, what others think you are. Third, there is your reflected image, what you think others think you are. There could be a fourth level, the real self, what you really are, yet such is usually unknown and may not even exist. Although what others think of you is very important—and what you think others think of you is certainly powerful in shaping your attitudes, feelings, and actions—what is really of greatest significance is what you think of yourself. Especially when it comes to change, how you perceive yourself will be the key.

However, perception involves more than one's self. Perception controls our vision of others, life, the world, and even reality itself. We can perceive others to be either friendly or hostile, acceptable or unacceptable, valuable or worthless. We can perceive life to be either a joyful challenge or a harsh burden. Our vision of life may be either optimistic or pessimistic. We can perceive the world around us as either relatively safe or terribly threatening. Some envision the world as "this is my Father's world," to quote one religious songwriter who saw the world as basically good, while others perceive the world to be "the devil's domain," full of evil and sin and rapidly catapulting itself into hell.

Some perceive reality objectively, a mix of both good and bad, right and wrong, difficult yet inviting. Others perceive reality as a nightmare or as a fantasy, with the former resulting in a lot of depression and the latter producing a lot of personal irresponsibility.

Evangelical Christians believe that the internalizing of authentic biblical faith, centered in God's revelation of himself in Jesus Christ, tends to produce a healthy and balanced perception of self, others, life, the world, and reality. This book is an attempt to guide the reader toward such a perception.

Christian faith seeks to guide the believer toward a certain quality of perception: perceiving according to the mind of Christ. The perception that most of us have is so often distorted by culture and experience. A personal and vital relationship with Jesus Christ, evangelical Christians testify, makes possible and tends to produce a perception of self, life, and reality that is in harmony with God's original plan for each of us. Jesus' invitation to two of his disciples on one occasion is certainly suggestive in a broader sense in this regard than originally intended: "Come . . . and you will see" (John 1:39). Following Jesus Christ provides one with an authentic perception of self and reality.

In addition, perception involves evaluation as well as description. By evaluation is meant some kind of emotional response to what is seen. If I see myself as ugly, I may feel repelled by myself. If I see myself as a loser, I might feel disgusted or sorry for myself. If I perceive myself as "dumb" or "stupid," I may feel justified in often saying, "I don't like me because I don't like stupidity," or at least, "Stupidity in my case is inexcusable, given all the wonderful opportunities I've had."

Perception usually evolves into some kind of approval or disapproval, acceptance or rejection. If I like myself, to some degree I will probably approve of my performance. I give myself permission to give myself certain strokes of approval. If I perceive certain others as "out to get me," I will in all likelihood respond by rejecting them. They will probably respond to my rejection by avoiding or criticizing me, which will in turn "prove" that my perception was correct in the first place. This emotional evaluation then provides a sort of double kickback in harmony with my descriptive perception. It doesn't matter whether or not my perception is correct, since the emotional evaluation tends to confirm its accuracy.

Perception is never total or complete. There are unknown elements regarding one's self. This is especially true with regard to the interaction we have with others in our arena of experience and influence. The self is always seen in relation to others. We are social creatures. Some aspects of the self are open to everyone, including oneself. Some are known only to ourselves. Some parts of the self are hidden to ourselves but known to others, while there is that segment of the self that is hidden to both oneself and others, that deep reservoir of the subconscious that seldom if ever comes to the surface but still plays a role in our behavior and attitudes in some unknown way.

The familiar "Johari Window" pictures this complex view of the self:

The Johari Window

Others

		Known	Unknown
Self	**Known**	Known to Self and Others	Known to Self but Unknown to Others
	Unknown	Unknown to Self but Known to Others	Unknown to Both Self and Others

Reflections from Others

I am sure there are many times in your life when you heard someone ask, as you were discussing some decision you were about to make or some planned action on your part, "But what will people say?" Or, "If you do that, what will others think of you?" The person doing the asking may have been yourself. The "reflected appraisals" of others have been a very formative influence in everyone's life. Who are these "people," these "others"? In most cases, they are relatives or close friends, the "significant others" in our lives. The most influential other people are usually our parents, especially the mother in our early years, and this will be discussed more fully in the next chapter.

But, for now, it is sufficient to say that what we think others think of us, how we believe they see us—the appraisals of our behavior we get from these "significant others"—directly affects our perception. Reflections from others become the spectacles through which we see ourselves.

Harry Stack Sullivan, a prominent psychiatrist and social-science theorist, suggested that our self-appraisals have their beginnings in our interpersonal relationships, especially within the family circle. The way we evaluate ourselves tends to come from "reflected appraisals." If a child is accepted, approved, respected, and loved for what he or she is, that child will most likely acquire an attitude of self-acceptance, self-respect, and even self-love. However, if the significant people in your life, especially those in the family, criticize, blame, put-down, and reject you in childhood, you are likely to develop heavily unfavorable attitudes toward yourself.

Simply put, as you are judged by others, so you will tend to judge yourself. Moreover, the attitudes you develop toward yourself will shape your attitudes toward others. You judge yourself as you have been judged and then, in turn, you judge others as you judge yourself. The bottom line for all this is: select your parents and other family members very carefully!

Of course, though you can't go back in time and select your family, you can do a lot to carefully select your current closest friends and other significant people in your life. Their reflected appraisals of what you think, say, and do continue to influence the perception you have of yourself. This is especially true if their appraisals confirm your longstanding vision of yourself.

Evangelical Christians believe that there is one Significant Other (God in Christ, as revealed in Scripture) whose appraisal of the believer has a powerful transforming effect upon the reshaping of his or her self-image. (This will be discussed in greater detail in a later chapter.)

Definition of the Situation

Several decades ago, W. I. Thomas, a famous American sociologist, set forth this theory: "If a person defines a certain situation as real, it will be real in its consequences." In other words, if you perceive a certain situation as a potentially rewarding or happy one, in all likelihood it will be. That is, we respond not only to the objective facts or features of a situation, but also to the perceived meaning the situation has for us.

Once the meaning has been assigned, it serves to determine not only one's behavior but also some of the consequences of that behavior. A circular process seems to take place: perception ("definition") determines meaning, and meaning confirms perception. In addition, perception determines consequences.

For example, a student who has the intellectual ability to pass an examination may be convinced that he is destined to fail. Being anxious, the student spends more time worrying than studying, since his mind is preoccupied with thoughts of failing the test. Consequently, he takes the exam and does fail. He perceived the situation as a failing one and subconsciously worked to produce the consequence.

Mary and Phil Smaltz came to me for marriage counseling. It did not take long to discover that Mary had such a poor self-image that she had defined her marriage as a failure almost from the beginning. Phil was such a wonderful person: caring, thoughtful, considerate, and a good provider. Deep inside, Mary perceived herself as not worthy of such a good husband. With her subconscious mind fast at work to confirm her perception of self, she often would unintentionally do things to irritate Phil. His patience began to wear thin. Arguments resulted. This confirmed to Mary that her marriage was a failure. In time, she proved her definition of the situation was true.

In the sixteenth century, Michel de Montaigne, the French essayist, wrote, "A man is hurt not so much by what happens as by his opinion of what happens." Much earlier (around the end of the first century A.D.), the Greek Stoic philosopher Epictetus observed, "Men are disturbed not by things but by the views which they take of them." And it was Shakespeare, in *Hamlet,* who wrote, "There is nothing either good or bad, but thinking makes it so." It is a common maxim that the situation itself is not what makes us happy or sad, but the way in which we respond to it. If you define yourself to be a loser, watch out: you will try to prove it's true. While, if you define yourself to be a winner, you will set in motion a series of actions that will in all probability result in some kind of success.

One psychological school of thought known as Rational Emotive Therapy conveys a similar idea in that advocates such as Robert Harper and Albert Ellis suggest several "irrational beliefs" that function in a deterministic way to produce certain behavioral consequences. One example of an irrational belief is: "Unless I am liked or approved by everyone, life is awful and I am a failure." Holding to such a belief is surely setting oneself up for failure, because there is no way anyone can be liked or approved by all

people around them. What you think or believe does have a powerful effect upon your life. That old adage, "It doesn't matter what
you believe as long as you are sincere," is psychological and behavioral baloney.

The Self-Fulfilling Prophecy

The "definition of the situation" is clearly a self-fulfilling
prophecy. Perception is a psychological form of prophesying. Unfortunately, so much of the time the beginning definition is a false
one. The resulting consequences never would have come into being in the absence of the faulty definition, or prophecy. However,
after acceptance of the incorrect perception, new actions are
evoked that make the originally false state of affairs come true.
Strangely, but truly, there is no conspiracy to make the definition
come true. Rather, the fulfillment of the prophecy occurs subtly
and unintentionally as the definer acts as if it were true, in accor-
dance with the belief.

The power of the self-fulfilling prophecy can be observed in the
area of race relations. Many whites define blacks as inferior, igno-
rant, immoral, worthless, and so on. Such a definition is deeply
rooted in American culture. Many people, both white and black,
accept this faulty definition as reality. The resultant behavior (discrimination on the part of whites, and surrender to the idea on the
part of blacks) "proves" the "truth" of the definition. The glaring
and numerous exceptions are usually ignored. Stereotyping
results: all blacks are considered inferior. The saddest thing about
all this is the large number of black children who buy into and
accept the definition, which results in a very poor self-image,
which in turn results in poor performance in school, home, work,
and community. The "exceptions" usually reject the original definition, redefine themselves in positive terms, and move on to
prove that they are persons of worth.

What you think of yourself—how you perceive yourself, what
value or worth you place upon yourself, what vision you hold of
yourself—is all-determinative in regard to what kind of person
you turn out to be, how you experience life, what your behavior
will be, what you will do with yourself vocationally, and what kind
of relationships you will have with others.

Labeling Theory

What do you call yourself? What terms do you use to describe
yourself when asked, "What kind of person are you?" There is
an important body of thought in social science called "labeling
theory." This has been applied considerably in studies related to
juvenile delinquency and criminology that seek to explain how
homes in particular and society in general produce delinquents
and criminals. It can also be applied to "normal" human growth
and development.

From the very beginning of life, humans are labeled in a variety
of ways: male or female, rich or poor, healthy or sick, big or little,
pretty or ugly, fat or skinny, and so on, although the extremes of
some of these labels do not exactly apply. Certain physical characteristics may stand out: a flaming red-headed infant will probably
be called "Red" by some in the family. An extremely small baby
may be labeled the "runt" in the family. A curly-headed child may
be tagged "Curly." And on and on we could go. In time, as a child
grows up, certain behavioral traits are noticed, sluggish or hyper-
active, brilliant or dull, introverted or extroverted, fast or slow,
artistic or athletic, to illustrate again with some extremes. Appropriate labels are then applied by significant others in the family or
peer group. Sometimes, without any consideration of the facts,
certain value judgments are made and applied to children. Some
of these are often negative and unfair, even cruel: stupid, dumb,
bad, dirty, ugly, good-for-nothing, creep, immoral, cheap, loser,
and more. In the opposite direction, positive and affirming labels
can be applied: smart, brilliant, good, clean, pretty, beautiful,
handsome, thoughtful, kind, loving, valuable, marvelous, wonderful, competent, winner, fine, for example.

The point here is that the person accepts certain labels from
these significant others and applies them to him or herself. Whatever labels we accept for ourselves become an intricate part of the
fabric of our personality, so much so that we feel compelled to
prove that such labels are true and accurate descriptions. For example, if you accept the label of "loser," you will subconsciously
work to show by your behavior and attitudes that you are, in fact,
a loser. Such a response then confirms your self-image. A large
part of the dynamics behind proving the accuracy of one's labels
is the very strong need every human being has to "belong." We

learn to belong by winning the approval of the significant others who have labeled us in various ways.

Some evangelical Christians are now recognizing the importance of labeling theory for Christian discipleship. If it is true that the way to change your behavior and attitudes is by changing your self-image labels, it stands to reason that growth and development in the Christian life would involve some kind of God-initiated and -directed re-labeling process. A close examination of the New Testament in the light of labeling theory has convinced many evangelicals that this is exactly what God seeks to do when a person accepts Jesus Christ as his or her personal Savior.

The New Testament presents a new set of labels for the believer's self-image. Paul's vivid analogy of taking off the clothes of the "old self" (before one becomes a Christian) and putting on the clothes of the "new self" (after one becomes a Christian) illustrates this process of re-labeling (Eph. 4:22–24; Col. 3:9–10). All of the terms describing a believer in Christ in the New Testament are labels to be internalized into the believer's new self-image. The old negative labels (the person as rebellious sinner) are to be replaced by the new positive labels (the person as obedient and trusting child of God).

This is one reason why it is so absolutely necessary for the Christian to engage in daily Bible reading and study if he or she is to grow as a believer. The Christian life is an ongoing process of replacing the old labels with the new biblical labels. Who and what I am as a Christian are therefore determined by a process of saturation in biblical revelation: the Word of God, in the hands of the Spirit of God, determines and shapes my new self-image in Christ, which in turn molds and directs my new behavior as a follower of Jesus Christ. Labeling theory simply helps us understand a little better the plan God set forth centuries ago for growing and developing his people in Christian character. (This process will be discussed in greater detail in a later chapter.)

Self-Esteem

As we have seen, self-image refers to the way you see yourself. But taking a good look at yourself needs to go beyond the cognitive dimension to the feeling dimension, which is described by the term *self-esteem,* the way you feel about yourself as perceived by your "self." If you see yourself as a "loser," you will probably feel bad about yourself. If you see yourself as a "winner," you will likely feel good about who you are. The feeling dimension provides the dynamic for confirming the accuracy of the way you see yourself. The "loser," in fact, becomes a loser because the bad or negative feelings drive the behavioral engine that carries one toward the losing consequences.

It is possible to identify two types of self-esteem: earned and conferred. Earned self-esteem comes from personal effort and accomplishments. This flows from one's work, career, skills in various areas, and achievement. Conferred self-esteem is unearned and comes from innate traits or personality characteristics, those elements received at birth, conferred by one's genetic heritage. Self-esteem can also be conferred by one's significant others and can come from cultural and social status. Being the child of prominent and respected parents in the community may confer good self-esteem, while being the child of poor, uneducated, lower-class parents, especially from a racially despised minority group, may confer poor self-esteem.

Both achieved and conferred self-esteem are important in the normal development of one's personality. A problem may develop when one depends on any one source for total self-esteem, such as the family's social status or one's ability to produce on the job. Financial reversals for the family or unexpected poor health could then destroy one's total self-esteem overnight. A more permanent source of self-esteem is that conferred by God within the very core of one's personality through a vital faith in Jesus Christ. Such self-esteem comes from neither personal achievement nor social status but from a relationship. When all other sources evaporate through unpredictable circumstances, this one remains.

Self-esteem is essentially rooted in feelings of self-worth and self-acceptance. When I perceive myself to be a person of worth and can accept myself unconditionally, I will more likely feel good about myself. On the other hand, if I see myself as a person lacking in value and can accept myself only when I perform well or live up to certain high standards imposed upon me (by others or myself), I will not likely feel good about myself very often.

Self-worth and self-acceptance are probably more cognitive than affective. That is to say, my worth and acceptability are

based upon rationally perceived information (e.g., "I am made in
the image of God, and I am a person so loved that Christ died for
me"), rather than based on subjective feelings that could fluctuate
under certain conditions or experiences of life. God's declaration
of my value is more important than how I happen to feel about
myself at any one time.

In the absence of self-esteem, there will probably be self-
negation, even self-hate. Certain segments of American culture,
especially those influenced by the teachings of some churches, actually encourage a depreciation of the self. Warnings against
pride, arrogance, and egotism abound to the point that we are encouraged to put ourselves down, even reject ourselves. The self is
considered as something evil, to be kept under control.

This aspect of the self can be subtly seen in noticing various
types of distorted or false self-esteem. Felix Montgomery has
identified several types of fake esteem, all of which betray a lack
of feelings of self-worth:

1. Workaholic: seeks esteem primarily from earned sources,
   driving oneself to do more and more.
2. Perfectionist: cannot deal with failure in self or any other
   person, seeking esteem in everything being "just right."
3. Conformist: depends on others for evaluation and standards, working to live up to others' expectations in order to
   feel good about one's self.
4. Dictator: feels good only when in charge, adopting a "macho" image with a boss complex, and seeking "yes" people
   for companions. A very insecure person, finding esteem in
   control.
5. Clown: finds esteem through excessive attention-seeking,
   keeping up a "life of the party" image, using activity as a
   form of escape from responsible interpersonal relationships.
6. Martyr: possesses little self-identity, seeking esteem
   through rigid self-denial. This person could be a religious
   fanatic who feels too good for this world, seeking esteem
   through a persecution complex.
7. Rebel: esteem is found by showing superiority through a rejection of normal, customary behavior. Since rebellion is
   different, the rebel is "special." This is a form of attention-

seeking behavior. [From Felix Montgomery, "Understanding Self-Esteem," *Church Administration*, December 1982, pp. 27–28.]

Persons with emotional health find their self-esteem in who they are as persons in their own right, realizing both their strengths and weaknesses. Persons with low self-esteem, on the other hand, tend to evade self-awareness, acting according to what others believe and expect. Their behavior is designed to win the approval of others. Such approval then substitutes for genuine self-love. This is actually a form of self-hate.

Is self-love permissible for a Christian? Jesus thought it was not only permissible but also necessary and desirable. He taught that you should love your neighbor "as yourself" (Matt. 22:39), and the idea originated with God's command to Moses in Leviticus 19:18. If God himself decreed that self-love is normal and natural, then why do some evangelical Christians have such a hard time with the idea of self-love? If their doctrine of sin results in the depreciation of the self, why doesn't their doctrine of redemption produce an enhancement of the new self in Christ? By "self-love" I am referring to a wholesome acceptance and benevolent feeling toward one's own total personality as loved and graced by God in Christ. A person who is "in Christ" (2 Cor. 5:17) has every reason to feel good about him or herself. It is also healthy and transforming. It is God's road to self-esteem in the best sense.

To Sum It Up

Take a good look at your "self." You are what you see yourself to be. If you don't like what you see, then you need a change of vision. You need the help of a specialist in visionetics. You need help in self-affirmation in self-imaging the best.

The self is YOU. The self observes, analyzes, describes, values, evaluates, judges itself and reality. The self is living. It reflects upon itself as both subject and object, which is one reason the human being is so unique. The self is the thinking, feeling, communicating, and acting expression of the whole person.

To know who you are you will need to understand all of these aspects of the self. Taking a good look at yourself, what do you see? Why do you see yourself that way? That is the question we will seek to answer next.

2

Why Do You See Yourself the Way You Do?

Remember that this book is about vision, your inner vision, a study in visionetics. You might call it psychological and sociological ophthalmology and optometry. Since the way you see yourself has such a direct influence upon your behavior, I think it is very important to know why you see your "self" the way you do. How did you get your current inner vision? Of course, this is related directly to the origin of the self. How did that self come into being? How was it shaped? Where did it get its content? The answers to these questions will also be of special interest to parents of young children.

Sociologists call this the process of "socialization," the dynamics of becoming a human being. This has been described as the "process of social interaction in which the individual acquires those ways of thinking, feeling, and acting essential for effective participation within society."[1] Those early-day pioneers of soci-

1. James W. Vander Zanden, *Sociology: A Systematic Approach* (New York: Ronald Press, 1965), pp. 242–43.

ology, Robert Park and Ernest Burgess,[2] declared, "Man is not born human. It is only slowly and laboriously, in fruitful contact, co-operation, and conflict with his fellows, that he attains the distinctive qualities of human nature." The process of becoming a human being never stops. Humans are always in the process of "becoming." But it does have a beginning, primarily in the social matrix of the family.

Helen Bird came for counseling with serious marital difficulties. She had what I call a V.I.P. Syndrome (see chapter 4). She saw herself as such a very important person that she felt she deserved a constant show of attention and recognition from everyone around her, especially her husband. Helen craved being the central attraction in all of her interpersonal relationships.

How did Helen develop this kind of personality? In her case it was largely due to having grown up as an only child who received an unusual amount of attention and recognition in her immediate as well as extended family. She was her parents' only child as well as her mother's parents' only grandchild. She grew up being showered with attention and reminders of her importance. Over the years, she grew to expect this from everyone.

Lewis, the man Helen married, did not realize the extent to which Helen expected recognition. He was so busy developing a career in his engineering profession that he tended to ignore Helen's need for attention. At least that's the way she felt— ignored and thus unimportant. The result: misery. The roots of Helen's marital problems reached back into her earliest childhood years. Her early development of a V.I.P. Syndrome set her up for serious disappointments as a married adult whose husband did not meet her envisioned personality needs.

An Early Start

Although not a cure-all, I believe that it helps to know something of the origin of one's self-image. The science of human growth and development strongly suggests that the shaping of the self begins even before one is born. There are definite prenatal influences—genetic, biological, chemical, psychological—that work to mold and fashion the structure of one's self.

2. Robert E. Park and Ernest W. Burgess, *Introduction to the Science of Sociology* (Chicago: University of Chicago Press, 1921), p. 79.

Peggy Mills came for counseling after several unhappy, even tragic, relationships with men. She clearly had a very poor and negative self-image. Peggy was bright, alert, sensitive, affectionate, and an extremely talented artist. She had a lot of reasons to feel good about herself. Her major "flaw" was her small size: 4 feet 9 inches tall and weighing 85 pounds. All of her "feminine" features were very attractive; she was indeed a very beautiful young woman. Yet she saw herself, as she put it, "an ugly runt." Her father's height was 6 feet, her mother's 5 feet 4 inches. Her two brothers were 5 feet 9 inches and 5 feet 11 inches, respectively. Somehow Peggy felt she had been cheated biologically.

Peggy was always the smallest among her peers at school. Actually, her girlfriends in high school tended to be taller than average, making her feel even smaller than she was. At times she would be teased about her size, which merely irritated her even more. Even in her twenties, when she would go shopping in a department store, the clerks would misread her age and suggest that she go to the children's department. This angered her immensely.

Because of her petite size and the real and imagined social responses of rejection to her smallness, Peggy developed a very negative attitude toward herself. She perceived herself to be "ugly" and even "repulsive." What boy would be attracted to a "runt"? What man would want to marry a "midget"?

Several pediatricians suggested to Peggy's parents that her poor self-image was related to her response to her small size, which was simply the product of her genetic heritage (there were small women in her family background) and possibly her biological development (which might have been blocked by unknown physical and chemical factors in her prenatal growth and development). Later cultural and social experiences simply made the situation worse.

A similar story could be told by people who are extremely overweight, or unusually tall, or in some other way do not approximate an "average" size or physical appearance. Our self-image is often the result of the way we respond to our physical features, something we have very little control over.

Choose Your Parents Carefully

If you want to guarantee a strong and healthy self-concept, then choose your parents carefully! Naturally, this is an impossibility, but the thought does emphasize the fact that your mother and father make the most important contribution to the development of your self-image. The family unit is the primary social matrix of the shaping of one's self, and parents are the major participants in that formative influence. This can also be illustrated with a negative case study.

Gary was born in the worst days of the 1930s Great Depression to parents struggling to make ends meet in a family business. Gary was the third child, and his mother's comment upon learning of her pregnancy tells it all: "The last thing I need in all this world is another baby!" Reba's nine months of pregnancy was a time of seething resentment toward her husband for getting her pregnant and toward the baby itself for interfering with their already difficult life. Besides, she felt deeply negative toward sex, and this unwanted pregnancy simply confirmed her negativity. The problem of sex, as Reba saw it, "only creates more problems."

Reba's feelings of rejection toward the unwanted baby mounted during her pregnancy. Some medical scientists today believe that such feeling can have a harmful effect upon the infant during these prenatal months. In other words, there is a sense in which the child can feel the rejection of the mother. Whether or not this can be proven, rejection by a mother will certainly be sensed after the birth of the child.

Reba was a religious, church-going woman and did not want others to think that she did not want this child. So she was good at putting up a pretense of acceptance and love, but deep inside, subconsciously, Reba's rejection of Gary came through in a variety of ways. Gary's father, Fred, was too busy trying to make a living to make up for his wife's lack of love for this third child. After all, he reasoned, the mother is supposed to raise the children!

Consequently, Gary grew up with a heavy rejection syndrome, feeling unloved, unwanted, and unworthy of anyone's acceptance. Gary spent the rest of his life looking for the love and acceptance he never got at home. However, since he saw himself as "rejectable," his behavior was a concerted effort to prove that he was, in fact, rejection-worthy. Therefore, in his adult years he wasted a lot of energy setting himself up to be rejected both at work and in his marriage. This was what brought Gary to counseling. His wife's love was "never enough," and even his own children "really do not love me," he would often say.

As a middle-aged adult, Gary was still seeing himself through the reflected appraisal of his mother: "You are unwanted and unloved." Slowly and painfully, Gary learned to "grace" and accept himself as a person of worth and significance.

Family Environment

Obviously, one's family is determinative in the growth and development of both the self and the self-image. In addition to the direct influence of early parent-child interaction, there is the molding power of the total family environment, which can be described as one's "self-image factory."

By *family environment* is meant the total atmosphere (mental, emotional, relational, physical, and spiritual) experienced in the home. This includes all of the interpersonal relationships (including husband-wife, parent-child, siblings, grandparents, uncles, aunts, cousins, in-laws) found in both the nuclear and extended family. *Environment* refers to attitudes, feelings, tones of voice, facial expressions, thoughts expressed, goals or objectives sought, resources available or lacking, time spent together, depth of relating, expectations, hopes and dreams envisioned, quality and character of authority, manner of coping with problems and crises, sense of togetherness, as well as the degree of acceptance of each other as persons of worth. The nature and quality of one's family environment will greatly determine what one's self-image will be.

Becky came for counseling because, as she said, "It seems that I'm driving everyone crazy at my house." Personality-profile tests revealed that Becky was a rigid perfectionist. Everyone and everything had to be "just right" in order to meet her approval. Becky was obsessed with keeping a clean house, which was never clean enough for her even after an all-day cleaning job by professionals. As she put it, her husband and children never dressed properly, never looked their best, never behaved like she expected. Actually, no one could live up to her standards.

How did Becky get this way? Several factors played a role, but her childhood family environment was revealing. She grew up in a home that was cold, both physically and emotionally. Love from her parents was generally conditional: "We love you if . . . ." Her parents were low-income people, but they had a deep sense of pride that "We're as good as other folks." This message came through loud and clear a million times while Becky was growing up, but it really communicated just the opposite. And so she learned that to be accepted by others she had to be "perfect—with everything and everyone just right and proper." With such a perfectionistic self-image, Becky was truly driving everyone around her crazy. Her neurosis was the product of her early family environment.

Childhood Experiences

The self is also shaped by a variety of early-childhood experiences. In addition to one's genetic inheritance, the way your parents treat you, and the atmosphere of one's family environment, your own unique personal experiences in childhood play a major role in the formation of the self, especially according to how you responded to those experiences.

According to psychiatrist Alfred Adler, the experiences one has in the context of the family constellation provide the most powerful influence in what kind of person one becomes. *Family constellation* refers to the position of each member of the family in relation to all the others. In addition to the unique position of the father and mother, there are the special positions of the children with reference to their birth order. (The reader is referred to an excellent popular treatment of this fascinating subject by Kevin Leman entitled *The Birth Order Book* [Revell, 1985].)

Birth-order studies are based upon thousands of cases in which general tendencies or trends of behavior and attitudes have been observed. For example, the first-born, or oldest, tends to be a sort of in-charge, responsible, and sometimes bossy person. The second-born tends to be competitive, striving to prove that he or she is as good and capable as the older sibling. The youngest, or "baby" of the family, tends to be "spoiled," a charmer, and one who expects others to do for him or her whatever needs to be done. A "middle child" may feel squeezed out or unloved or ignored. This child's behavior is often prompted by a deep inner question: "Does anyone out there love me?" An only child, obviously, has no experience with siblings, receives all of the parents' attention, and may therefore develop a V.I.P. Syndrome, which expects an unusual amount of attention and recognition. The only child tends not to develop as many skills in social interaction as do children in other ordinal positions. An only boy, for example, will tend to date girls later in life than other boys. He (or she) may be something of a loner.

Remember that these are general tendencies and that there are exceptions to the "rules." Each person has his or her unique personality characteristics, but birth order plays a significant role in shaping the self. The reason for this, according to Adler, is that the basic drive of the human being is the need to belong. Each one in the family is striving to make a place for him or herself. The way the individual achieves a sense of place or belonging is determined considerably by birth order. One's birth order, or ordinal position in the family, provides the raw material for the psychological "sculpturing" of the self. This theory does not tell the whole story of the formation of the self, but it does provide a major insight into some of the forces at work in the process of becoming the human being that you do become.

Our childhood experiences also include events that precipitate the several reflected appraisals we receive during our early years. Some of the most important value judgments about us are communicated by significant others in our early childhood during specific events in our formative years. One young woman who came to me for counseling was deeply scarred when she was abandoned at age four by her divorced mother. This event climaxed a relationship that convinced her that she was not worth loving or keeping. One of my students in his early thirties still vividly remembered his first-grade teacher's assigning each child to draw something with a crayon. When the teacher looked at his drawing, she bluntly said, "That's the ugliest picture I've ever seen. Can't you do any better than that?" Such a comment simply reinforced the boy's already-poor self-image. As an adult, he said he remembered it as though it had happened yesterday. Our early memories often symbolically explain how our self-image was shaped. This will be discussed in detail later, when we present a method for changing one's self-image.

Persons with a strong and positive self-image usually have an abundance of childhood experiences that involve love, affirmation, encouragement, and faith. One of my earliest preschool memories is of my father teaching me how to count. In our family grocery store, farmers would bring their eggs to trade for groceries. We would transfer the eggs from buckets to egg cartons or cases. When I protested that I couldn't count, Dad responded, "Sure you can; I'll teach you how." This type of affirmation happened many times during my early years as he taught me various things about the business. Since he always exuded confidence in me, I knew he believed in me. Such early experiences helped to give me a positive self-image.

The Looking-Glass Self

Another way of understanding why you see yourself the way you do is to examine early-day sociologist Charles Horton Cooley's theory of the "Looking-Glass Self." First, remember that the self may be defined as the person as perceived by that person in a socially determined frame of reference or a social context of interpersonal relationships. One's "person" is both subject and object. That is, we can reflect upon ourselves, something that no other creature on the face of the earth can do, so far as we know. Within our mind's eye, we can take a position on the outside of ourselves and view our thoughts, feelings, and behavior within the context of a socially acquired frame of reference. This means that an essential characteristic of the self is its reflexive character.

I believe that the self is a unique creation. God provides the raw materials and the possibilities or potential, and the family, the culture, and society (usually expressed in a local community) work with the person's own will, choices, and responses to determine the quality of being that the self becomes. You are the result of all of these forces working together for good or for ill. (As an evangelical Christian, I also believe that man's sin nature plays havoc with God's original plan for man, and this will be discussed in a later chapter.) Gradually a sense of self-awareness develops, involving one's physical, mental, and emotional makeup.

Quite early, the human being develops the marvelous power of the imagination. Notice that the word *image* is in that term. We learn to "image" reality, whether past, present, or future. Cooley theorized that human beings become both subject and object to themselves by temporarily assuming the position of other people, looking at themselves, as it were, through others' eyes. This is an ever-recurring process going on in each of our minds, characterized by three separable phases:

Phase one. We imagine how we appear to other people. Here we imagine how other people perceive us. If I have a torn shirt, I imagine that this is what others see when they view me.

Phase two. We imagine how others judge our appearance. Here we imagine how others interpret or evaluate what they have seen. How will some people judge a torn shirt? I might assume that some will think that I got my shirt torn in a fight. Since getting into fights is not exactly a virtue, I might conclude that others will evaluate me negatively in this regard. Actually, most others will simply overlook my torn shirt, but I nevertheless imagine how others are evaluating my behavior. My interpretation need not be correct; it may even be in error.

Phase three. We experience some kind of emotion with reference to what we regard to be others' judgment of us. On the basis of the processes in phases one and two, we may experience fear, sympathy, pity, anger, love, contempt, embarrassment, envy, pride, or some other emotional response. In the case of the torn shirt, I may experience embarrassment or perhaps anger that others could be so "unfair," since I actually got my shirt torn by a nail protruding from a wall where I happened to walk by.

Although the process involved in the Looking-Glass Self is ever recurring, we usually are not explicitly or consciously aware of its taking place, since it occurs more or less in the subconscious mind. Yet, under some circumstances, we could be very much aware of the process, especially when we are sensitive to what kind of impression we are making. A child visiting his grandparents may feel extremely self-conscious. He may wonder, "What are they thinking of me? Do they love me? Are they proud of me? Do they think I am stupid or smart?"

Although the ideas involved in the Looking-Glass Self are most appropriate and insightful, the process can be misleading. The theory does not imply that our self-concept changes radically every time we confront a new person or face a new social experience. Rather, the accumulation of experience usually builds up an increasingly definite and stable self.

Significant Others

The Looking-Glass Self works best in the presence of the significant others in our lives. I have already referred to this concept several times. Who are these people? How do they function in our lives?

Obviously, during the earliest stages of the development of the self, the most influential significant others in one's life are the parents, especially the mother. Of course, significant others are "significant" to a particular person for several reasons. One is by definition: we define certain persons as significant, primarily because of the nurture and support they provide. Another is due to proximity: these people are close and available and meet our most immediate needs. Consequently, from them we receive a strong sense of identity as well as some degree of self-esteem. They make us feel important, providing us with a sense of worth.

Significant others function on our behalf in several ways: (1) they provide a value system, something all humans must have in order to become functional in society; (2) they give emotional support, which keeps us motivated and going forward in growth; (3) they help us make a place for ourselves in the family, which meets our primary need to belong; and (4) they teach us how to internalize the culture in our personalities, which makes it possible for us to relate to other humans in our society in some meaningful way.

The number of significant others increases in our lives as we continue to grow. Brothers and sisters, grandparents, aunts and uncles, and other relatives soon come into the picture of influence. Close friends of the family, church leaders such as a pastor or Sunday-school teacher, as well as influential schoolteachers may also join the circle of significant others. Their reflected appraisals as perceived by the individual continue to be a shaping influence on one's life.

Probably the most important influence exerted upon the self by significant others is in the area of values. What is your attitude toward money, property, people, time, work, play, sex, marriage and family, integrity, the future, and so on? The way you value these things was learned by you from your significant others. They taught you by word and example the priorities you have adopted in your life. In other words, you find your own significance in who you are and what you do in the perceived example of the significant others in your life.

Reference Groups

Another powerful force to understand in explaining why you see yourself the way you do is the "reference group," of which there are probably several in your life. A reference group is a group "that provides the standards and perspective regulating an individual's behavior within a given context, regardless of whether one is a member of the group or not."[3]

Examples of reference groups could include a sports team, a military unit, a church or denomination, a labor union, a political party (even on a local level), a work group at one's place of employment, a civic club, or a peer group in the school or community. In some crowded urban communities, gangs are often powerful reference groups for adolescents. On college campuses, especially residence schools, several reference groups may be found, such as a fraternity or sorority.

Studies show that people who join a church for the first time must engage in a process of both disattachment from previous reference groups of a more secular character as well as attachment to the new church reference group, which espouses religious values. If this process does not take place, the new member will in all likelihood not remain active long in the church's life and activities. This can be a real problem for evangelical Christians, who are taught to be "in the world" but not "of the world." The strongest and most committed evangelicals tend to be those who learn early how to balance separation and penetration in their witness ministry. But their primary commitment is to their new reference group, the local church and its fellowship.

A reference group is a powerful molder of the human personality, providing one with moral standards and life perspectives that regulate and shape one's behavior. Changing one's behavior often calls for changing membership or identification regarding one's reference groups. Long after you leave your family of orientation, your reference groups continue to call the shots on how you believe, feel, and behave. This is true with both an actual membership group (an in-group) and those groups to which you aspire to belong and thus has only a psychological identification for you. The latter could be illustrated with the Ku Klux Klan, the Dallas Cowboys professional football team, the Roman Catholic Church, a campus fraternity with high social status, the characters on a daily-viewed television soap opera, or a Southern Baptist traveling mission-action group whose members spend their summer vacation time in Mexico building churches.

3. Vander Zanden, pp. 236–37.

For about two years my younger son, Todd, was a lowly enlisted man in the National Guard, but he aspired to membership among the commissioned officers. Through the R.O.T.C. program in his college he was commissioned a second lieutenant and today he is still an officer. This change involved taking on the values, attitudes, spirit, and ideas of commissioned officers.

Louise confided to me after several counseling sessions that watching daytime soap operas on television for several months contributed to her gradual disillusionment with her "drab" marriage, motivating her to look elsewhere for an "exciting man" in her life. Her unfaithfulness almost wrecked her marriage. Her husband assumed some of the responsibility in his overcommitment to his job, willingly forgave her, and sought to reprioritize his time at home and work. Yet Louise admitted that a television reference group had a lot to do with her changing values.

Individual Response

In addition to the above explanations and influences in the shaping of one's self and self-image, there is the individual's own response to circumstances, situations, persons, and groups. Since everyone responds differently and uniquely to a given situation, the element of "will" cannot be ignored. We are volitional creatures, and we can choose our responses in life. In many ways, we are the product of our choices as much as we are of the influences of others around us.

I remember reading *Manchild in the Promised Land* (Macmillan, 1965) by Claude Brown, who had grown up in a poor black ghetto with all the social and psychological cards stacked against him. Whereas most of his black peers went the route of poverty, hunger, and crime, Brown chose to head in a different direction, graduated from Howard University in Washington, D.C., and became a noted author at a crucial time during the Civil Rights Movement of the 1960s. To be sure, Claude Brown was an "exception," but he did break out of the rut of sociological determinism, where the great majority of his peers remained. Why? Individual response. He *chose* to be different. Why? No one knows for sure, not even Brown himself, but I like to think that he was open to the stirring of God in his heart to break out of the rut by making the appropriate choices.

Earlier we discussed Adler's theory regarding the family constellation and how one's ordinal position (birth order) plays a significant role in the shaping of one's personality. Each one of us has the driving need to belong. The circumstances of one's birth order in the family provide the raw materials for the development of the self. Yet, here too, the individual's own response is the key element. For example, usually the oldest child in the family responds with a strong sense of responsibility and learns a "take charge" lifestyle, but some first-born children are "dethroned" by a younger sibling and become passive, sickly, and dependent. Why? Individual response. Personal choice of response is simply one of those mysterious and unpredictable elements in human growth and development.

Harry Emerson Fosdick, the famous New York preacher of another generation, often emphasized in his books and sermons the significance of the power of one's volitional ability to choose to be different. Regardless of the limitations of one's family background and the problems and difficulties in one's early childhood environment, the individual can choose to be an exception to the rule. Almost every great person in history had several reasons for not succeeding. All of us could come up with many excuses for not becoming our best in life.

One of the loudest and clearest messages in the Bible speaks to this very point. By the grace of God, we do not have to give in to the negative circumstances of life, whether sickness, injury, poverty, a broken home, financial reversals, or personal tragedy of a variety of sorts. Rather, we can choose to allow the wisdom and power of God to redirect our lives toward a redemptive difference wherein we can become all that God ever intended for us to become. Yes, even poor and unwise choices of the past that have caused us to see ourselves with a negative self-image can be transformed into new and healthy choices that can result in the reformation of a positive self-image. (A later chapter will discuss how this can happen, even for a grown adult.)

To Sum It Up

Why do you see yourself the way you do? Perception is shaped by a variety of influences and decisions, largely in the context of the family. The shaping of the self begins quite early, even before birth. Your parents were the key figures in your journey toward becoming the human being you are today. Your family environment provided the atmosphere in which you were molded. Thousands of childhood experiences provided the raw materials for your self's development, especially as you bought the appraisals of several other people regarding your self-worth. Significant others and a variety of groups played major roles. And, finally, you made certain key decisions, choices that sent you up certain paths that partially explain your self-image. Therefore, both conditioning and choices played key roles in shaping your self-image. In the midst of it all, maybe God had something to do with it, either in your acceptance or your rejection of his will for the shaping of your life.

Is your perception of self basically positive or negative? The next two chapters will contrast these two possible perceptions. See if you can locate *your* self in the discussion.

3

The Positive Self-Image

You would think that everyone would want a positive self-image and high self-esteem. Surely we all would desire to feel good about ourselves. But life doesn't work out this way for a lot of people. Those of us who work with people and their personal problems in counseling can easily conclude that a large percentage of people in society have anything but a positive vision of themselves. Given the large number of books that have been published in recent years on the subject, it is quite clear that people are indeed hungry for a more positive self-image and higher self-esteem.

Earlier I suggested that a primary source of one's self-image is the cluster of labels people attach to themselves in early childhood. There is a whole reservoir of labels available in every family environment from which to choose. Consequently, the wide variety of possible self-images is the result of the large number of available labels provided by one's environment and experiences, particularly in the family setting. You will recall our discussion of labeling theory. A label refers to a personality characteristic or trait that is dominant and descriptive of what you see in yourself.

Some labels are positive, while others are negative. That is, some are constructive and complimentary, while others are destructive and negating of one's self-worth.

One's choice of labels is the consequence of both the influence of significant label-givers (those significant others in one's life) and the individual's own acceptance of certain labels and the rejection of others. Individual choice is equally as important as the reflected appraisals of others. When two people look out a window, one sees the beautiful sunset in the distant western sky, while the other sees the dirt on the window. Why? Individual choice. Both are free to see what they want to see. Of course, the dynamics behind the choices are not always clear, but one's volitional ability can choose different responses.

Some would argue that there is no such thing as "free will," that one's choices are determined by influences outside the person's own awareness or control. However, evangelical Christians presume from biblical teachings that everyone is responsible for his or her own choices and behavior. This presumption also implies that one is free to some degree to choose one's responses.

However, for now I want to stress the influence of the positive label-givers among one's significant others. Positive label-givers are also to be found among groups, belief systems, and institutions. These can be the molders of a positive self-image (or a negative one, for that matter).

Positive Label-Givers

Positive label-givers may be seen primarily as label-providers, for in the final analysis whatever labels we take to ourselves are chosen rather than forced upon us. Positive label-givers are generally persons who have a strong, positive self-image of their own. Now what do I mean by "positive"? The word may be defined as that which is marked by or indicating acceptance, approval or affirmation. If I possess a positive self-image, it means that I accept, approve, and affirm myself—just as I am. I love myself with a wholesome, realistic, and unconditional love. Positive label-givers are persons who—as significant individuals or leaders in the context of influential institutions, such as schools or churches—influence us to see ourselves as acceptable, approved, and affirmed. One's general environment can also be a positive label-giver.

A positive family matrix is probably the most powerful positive label-giver. It is interesting that "matrix" comes from the Latin word for womb, that which nurtures and finally gives birth to the total human person. A positive family matrix is one wherein the things said and done, the attitudes and feelings expressed, the beliefs and values shared, communicate to each person in the unit a deep sense of value, love, security, trust, freedom, confidence, and nurture. A child growing up in such a home is made to feel very important yet humble, capable yet realistic, free yet responsible, blessed yet one who blesses.

In most instances, you can walk into a home and before long detect whether the family atmosphere provides a matrix for the growth and development of a positive self-image. The condition and arrangement of the furniture, the cleanliness and orderliness of the rooms, the manner in which the house is heated or cooled, how the clothes are kept, the way the yard is cared for, the location of and procedure regarding family meals, the quality and appearance of the food served, the context and quality of family conversation, the tone of voice used to speak to each other, can all point to the belief and conviction that everyone in the family is highly prized and cherished.

For example, when the furniture is neatly arranged and comfortable to sit in or use; when the rooms are clean and orderly; when the house is adequately and comfortably heated or cooled; when the clothes are picked up and cared for with some kind of organization; when the yard is neatly trimmed and attractive, especially during the greener months; when at least one meal a day is eaten together around the dining table with wholesome conversation, each one contributing something from his or her own experience of the day; when the food served is attractive and nutritious and prepared by loving hands; when the content and quality of family conversation is meaningful, enjoyable, calm, nonjudgmental, and balanced between sharing and listening; when the tone of voice spoken is understanding, accepting, and pleasant—then such a family atmosphere encourages the growth and development of a positive self-image.

Positive label-givers are essentially encouragers, affirmers, and nurturers. My father encouraged me to see myself as valued, capable, responsible, and cooperative. My mother trusted me, and so I felt free. She also nurtured me with patience and tolerance, and so I felt emotionally secure. Some of my grade-school teach-

ers encouraged me to see myself with a realism that balanced
strengths with weaknesses, helping me to set achievable goals.
My sister has always affirmed my intelligence and competence,
and I learned to see myself as an achiever because she saw me that
way.

Positive "modeling" is another source of positive labels. If you
are surrounded by people who have strong, positive self-images,
and their behavior models such perception, you will tend to emu-
late their patterns of behavior. Watching my parents cope with the
dark days of the Depression in the 1930s and come through with
some measure of success taught me coping skills. I learned the
secret of survival during hard times: prayer, faith, and hard work.
I recall that as a small boy I often observed my father praying
alone in the back stockroom of our small grocery store just after
opening up around 7:00 A.M. He was obviously confident that God
would see him through those lean days. I learned from his example that I could also trust God to empower me through hard times.

Positive goal-setters are also providers of positive labels. Think
of the people who have encouraged you to set positive goals for
your life. If you were challenged to get a college education or a
trade-school diploma, you thereby sought to develop a marketable
skill and aim toward a successful career. Family members or
close friends may have encouraged you toward other positive
goals: marriage and a family or a productive single lifestyle, a
meaningful church life, active community involvement, making
new friends, establishing a good credit rating, seeking a job pro-
motion, or even involvement in community, state, or national politics as a civic duty to your country. Such goals imprinted upon
you the label of "achiever," and you bought it for yourself.

Alfred Adler believed that all behavior is goal-oriented. If this
be true, then establishing positive goals for one's life may propel
one to "go for it," which reinforces a positive self-image. As already discussed, our self-image and actions are influenced by the
labels we have to "prove" are true, and our goal-setting behavior
is part of the total picture.

Those who love us unconditionally are also positive label-
givers. When parents and other significant persons in our lives
love, accept, and support us spontaneously, with "no strings at-
tached," we tend to feel that we have an inherent value apart from
any performance. Love that has to be earned can also be lost or

taken away when our performance fails to measure up. Unconditional love sticks to us and gives us a sense of being "lovable" just as we are. Such love tells us that we have value, significance, and acceptance just for being who and what we are.

Unconditional lovers have offered to me such positive labels as "loved," "valued," "capable," "free," "secure," "attractive," and even "happy." In my judgment, Jesus Christ was the most unconditional lover who ever lived. No one had to earn his or her way into Christ's presence and fellowship. He accepted people just as they were. He came not to condemn but to save, and he did it with unconditional love: "I love you regardless of . . . ." "I love you in spite of . . . ." "I love you just the way you are." There was none of conditional love's "I love you if you are good [clean, perfect, moral, and so on]."

I have observed through the years that parents who express unconditional love tend to produce children who grow up with positive self-images. Likewise, I have observed that a husband or wife who demonstrates unconditional love toward his or her spouse tends to encourage that spouse to perceive him or herself in a more positive way. If you will stop trying to change your children or your spouse and instead express simple unconditional acceptance, you will begin to see some amazing miracles of transformation take place.

Even institutions can be positive label-givers. An example might be a school with "spirit," or pride, and administrators and teachers who instill confidence in each student's potential to learn and mature intellectually, emotionally, and socially. Numerous studies have shown that when a teacher communicates faith and positive expectations to a student, that student is much more likely to do well in school.

The church is another example of an institution that can provide positive labels. In my opinion, the gospel (which is, of course, positive), when preached by a positive church fellowship can do more to turn people around from a negative self-image to a positive one than any other force on earth. Unfortunately, I have discovered that a lot of people who have grown up in a family with a negative self-image also went to a church that strongly reinforced that negative perception of themselves. They heard numerous sermons and Bible lessons that communicated that "you are bad, worthless, dirty, sinful, ugly, vain, selfish, and good-for-nothing."

I certainly recognize that the Bible clearly teaches that every Christian has a sin problem, an old carnal nature with remaining vestiges, and is in this life imperfect. But the Bible also clearly teaches that the believer in Jesus Christ is a "new creation" (2 Cor. 5:17) whose life has been transformed by the power of God through the Good News of Jesus Christ. Because of the very presence of the crucified and risen Christ in the believer's life, he or she is a new person, a "new self" (Col. 3:9–10) who has every right to see that self with all of the positive labels commensurate with the nature and character of God. This does not mean that believers are "little gods," but rather that they may now reflect the very life of Jesus Christ, who has revealed the true nature and character of God (2 Cor. 4:1–6).

Christians need to recognize who they are "in Christ" and not be constantly reminded of their past sinful lives that are now "dead" (Rom. 6:6–11). Pastors and churches cannot positively motivate their people by constantly running them into the ground with messages about how bad or unworthy they are. Christians are encouraged to grow in their faith when they are reminded of who they are now "in Christ." Jesus affirmed his followers and never berated them. Their lives changed because he was a positive label-giver. They took on *his* new labels, which reflected the nature and character of God, and worked to prove they were true in their daily behavior. This is still God's plan for spiritual growth today.

Positive Labels

What are the basic positive labels that we may attach to ourselves so as to constitute and reinforce a positive self-image? Several of these have been alluded to previously, but now it is time to list and describe each of them. Remember that a label is also a behavioral goal toward which the person wearing it strives. Whatever we label ourselves has to be "proven" correct. What you see is what you do; you have to do this to maintain sanity and balance.

Notice also that there is a unity among the positive labels that constitutes a whole. Someone with a positive self-image will more than likely bear several of these labels. I am reminded of Paul's description of "the fruit of the Spirit" (Gal. 5:22–23). He does not say "fruits" (plural) but "fruit" (singular), as in a cluster of grapes, hanging together in a unity. The labels of the positive self-image work together in harmony to mold a stable personality, one that is well-rounded and balanced. There is strength in such unity.

1. "Loved"

The label of "loved" is primary, basic, and all-encompassing, to say the least. Ideally and hopefully, this label will be given at the earliest possible time in one's life, even before birth. Humanly speaking, it is life's greatest experience to know that you are loved. Although love comes to each of us on an action level (for example, love was something expressed by what our parents did to and for us as early as possible), it is experienced on a feeling level: we *feel* wanted, cherished, valued, and nurtured. This results in our feeling "lovable," that is, worth loving.

If I see myself as "loved," it is only natural for me to behave toward others in a loving manner. Loved people are good at loving others. Studies show that people who have good marriages characterized by a warm, loving relationship, as well as people who are loving parents toward their children, are those who were adequately loved as children when they were growing up at home. Those studies also show that we are generally able to love others only to the degree that we have been loved, primarily during the early years of life.

If I see myself as "loved," I perceive myself to be accepted, and thus acceptable. I maintain a vision of myself as one who has been "graced." The biblical concept of grace comes from God's action in Jesus Christ, who forgives and reconciles persons not on the basis of having been good enough but on the basis of God's unmerited love. Paul said that believers in Christ are saved by grace and not by works (Eph. 2:8–9). God accepts us on the basis of Jesus' death on the cross on our behalf. Grace is the consequence of God's unconditional love. Jesus' death proved that God unconditionally loves us just as we are (see Rom. 5:8). To be "graced" is to be accepted as you are. In turn, this enables you to accept other people as they are, warts and all. To be "graced" empowers you to be a "gracer." What you see is what you do.

2. "Valued"

Another positive label that flows out of the preceding one is "valued." Ideally, this label should also be applied at the earliest possible moment in life. To be valued means that you are of considerable and significant worth. You are prized and cherished beyond measure. Of course, no monetary figure can be placed on your value, for you are really priceless. Your worth is inestimable and outside the standards of gold, silver, dollars, or property. To be valued means that you are irreplaceable. Those who value you would never think of trading you in on a new model!

Closely associated with the "valued" label is the concept of "good," but not in a moral sense. I am suggesting here the idea of "good for something" as over against "good for nothing." Even Jesus shrank from the moral connotation of "good" when applied to himself (Luke 18:19), probably due to his natural humility. Rather, I am thinking of the way Jesus used the term in the parable that referred to the "good and faithful servant" (Matt. 25:21). Such goodness can refer to the high valuation you can accept for yourself if you have a personal, saving relationship with Jesus Christ. "In Christ" God sees the believer as "good" and not "bad," or "evil." The apostle Paul clearly teaches in his Epistle to the Romans that "in Christ" the believer is righteous before God. This "righteousness" comes from God by faith and refers to a right standing with God. God has thereby placed a new valuation upon you because of what Jesus Christ accomplished through his death and resurrection. (Read Romans 4:4–8, 25.)

The vision of self as "valued," or "good," functions to produce character and behavior that is valuable and "good for something." On the other hand, if your label is "marked down" and "cheap," your response will be consistent with it. What you see is what you do.

3. "Responsible"

A third positive label might be described as "responsible." This label takes time to apply to oneself, since it must be learned in relation to the expectations of other people. When I come to see myself as "responsible," I will strive to prove that I am a trustworthy, dependable, honest, and truthful person.

It appears to me that I learned to be a responsible person by being given responsibility and by being trusted to act responsibly. My parents gave me some basic responsibilities that were commensurate with my age at the time and trusted me to be trustworthy, dependable, honest, and truthful. I knew they believed that I would behave in a responsible manner, and I felt an inner compulsion to live up to their expectations. Maybe I wanted their approval, but I really felt the desire and possibly the need to measure up to the label of "responsible" that I had accepted. Both parents were good models of responsibility, and I liked the sense of security this gave our family. I saw strength in the label and sought the strength it provided.

The biblical call to faithfulness is directly related to the label of "responsible." Christ's faithfulness to his followers is the basic dependable model, even for wavering believers (2 Tim. 2:13). God's eternal faithfulness is an ongoing source of encouragement for each one to live responsibly (1 Cor. 1:9; 1 Thess. 5:24; Heb. 10:23). Christ's ultimate challenge to "be faithful, even to the point of death, and I will give you the crown of life" (Rev. 2:10) keeps us moving toward the goal of responsibility.

If you see yourself as "responsible," you must prove the truth of such vision with responsible behavior, such as being a dependable provider for your family, an accessible and understanding parent for your children, and a loving and faithful spouse for your wife (or husband). Again, the label becomes the goal toward which your behavior and attitudes aim.

4. "Capable"

A fourth positive label includes several positive traits of what might be called a resourceful personality: "capable." This self-vision projects a certain efficiency and ability for various performances or accomplishments. Sometimes we speak of such a person as having self-confidence. He or she is "sure-footed." This person is a "winner," we say.

The "capable" self-image reflects strength, achievement, optimism, competence, and intelligence. When you perceive yourself to be a "capable" person, you generally will not shrink from challenges, opportunities, or problems but will tackle them head-on, believing that you have the resources to deal constructively with them, or at least you will try to find the necessary resources.

The vision of "capable" gives one the courage and motivation to seek solutions for a problem-oriented marriage, to resolve parent-child conflicts, to rebuild bridges of understanding where communication in the family has broken down, to settle differences of opinion at home or at work with meaningful and agreeable compromise, and to achieve success in one's career when failure and defeat seemingly meet one at every turn.

The "capable" label sets before you such a positive goal that put-downs such as "loser," "dummy," "weakling," or "gloomy" are never applied to yourself. These are rejected as "not true of me." "Capable" self-perception builds such inner confidence that sometimes even cancer can be arrested in one's body (see Dr. Bernie Siegel's fascinating book, *Love, Medicine, and Miracles,* Harper & Row, 1986, for numerous illustrations). Such inner confidence is a winning attitude and can provide leadership to build great churches (the modern stories of Pastors John Bisagno of First Baptist Church of Houston, Texas, and Robert Schuller of The Crystal Cathedral in Garden Grove, California, are thrilling accounts of "possibility thinking"). Or it can pull faltering businesses out of the fires of failure into successful enterprizes (recently dramatized by the winning spirit of Chrysler's Lee Iaccoca). The "capable" label can also inspire missionaries to go into "impossible" situations and become the catalysts for hundreds of new churches (as in Tanzania and Kenya in East Africa in recent years). The "winner" will never be heard to repeat "The Seven Last Words of the Church"—"We've never done it that way before"—and back off from a difficult but challenging opportunity.

The Bible is full of examples of the "capable" person. Paul said, "I can do everything though him [Christ] who gives me strength (Phil. 4:13). And, "Forgetting what is behind and straining toward what is ahead, I press on toward the goal to win the prize for which God has called me heavenward in Christ Jesus" (Phil. 3:13b–14). Paul often referred to the sense of confidence he had because of his relationship with Christ (Eph. 3:12; Phil. 1:6). Paul was no weak-kneed "loser." Even in times of weakness, distress, and hardship, he found strength in the power of Christ in his life (2 Cor. 12:7–10). His new self-image in Christ gave him an inner vision of "capable," and his behavior proved it was a true perception.

In the Old Testament, the life stories of such notables as Abraham and Sarah, Isaac and Rebekah, Jacob and Rachel, Joseph, Moses, Joshua, Rahab, Ruth and Naomi, Deborah, Samuel, David, Elijah, Elisha, as well as the writing prophets whose personal lives we know something about, reveal men and women whose self-image bore the label of "capable." They saw themselves as persons of intelligence, vision, competence, achievement, spiritual strength, and faith-oriented optimism. Chapter 11 of the Book of Hebrews presents a list and some brief statements regarding several of those Old Testament "capables." Each was a "winner" because of God's help.

People who bear the label "capable" tend to succeed at productive jobs, have a strong marriage, maintain wholesome and enjoyable relationships with their children, become the strongest and most active supporters of their local church, and provide constructive and stable leadership for their community, state, and nation. These are the heroes and models who so often inspire the rest of us to live up to our potential and even join their ranks.

5. "Free"

Another positive label flows naturally out of both the spirit of American democracy and biblical faith: "free." To see yourself as "free" is to envision yourself as liberated from the arbitrary power and control of others. You sense the freedom to be yourself and not what someone else determines for you to be. The "free" self-image overlaps the perception of yourself as "responsible" and "capable." You rarely feel the need to be told what to do and how to do it. You are both "capable" and "free" to make your own decisions.

You are free from the bondage of culture's arbitrary demands and religion's legalistic requirements. You are free from external rules, whatever their source. You have the freedom to become the unique person ordered by your creation.

Some might argue that the "free" self-image is tantamount to selfishness, self-centeredness, and egotism, that its favorite song is "I Did It My Way," and that its basic philosophy is a sort of go-jump-in-the-lake attitude toward other people. Of course, there is always a certain amount of risk with freedom. It was Augustine who said, "Love and do what you will," and has been misunderstood ever since.

The inner vision of "free" I have in mind implies a responsible freedom that is sensitive toward the scruples and needs of others. What other people think is important but not to the degree of allowing their thoughts to dominate one's conscience. The apostle Paul was one of those persons who experienced in his relationship with Jesus Christ a liberty from legalistic regulations and meaningless rules regarding moral and cultural trivia. In Christ, Paul learned how to break free from religious "trivial pursuit." In his Epistle to the Romans (14:1—15:13), Paul shows us how to balance freedom with responsibility in our daily behavior. It is most interesting that when Paul describes those who are the most "freed-up" regarding religious and cultural do's-and-don'ts, he calls them "strong," while those with all kinds of trivial moral hang-ups are referred to as "weak." Yet the strong who are "free" are to be strong enough to choose not to offend unnecessarily the weak when the occasion calls for certain restraints (note especially Rom. 14:21 in context). The same principle is applied in Paul's First Epistle to the Corinthians regarding eating meat offered to idols (1 Cor. 8). Paul was truly the "apostle with the heart set free" (F. F. Bruce) as well as the great "apostle of liberty" (Richard Longenecker).

Becoming a Christian provides us with a perspective of seeing ourselves as "free." Paul reminded the Galatian believers: "It is for freedom that Christ has set us free. Stand firm, then, and do not let yourselves be burdened again by a yoke of slavery" (Gal. 5:1). Yet this spiritual and moral freedom should be exercised with responsibility, as he explained: "You, my brothers, were called to be free. But do not use your freedom to indulge the sinful nature; rather, serve one another in love" (v. 13). The label of "free" provides a positive goal that enables us to strive toward the exhilaration of liberation, where the moral and spiritual air we breathe is clean, brisk, and fresh.

6. "Secure"

A very significant positive label to wear on one's self-image is "secure." The word comes from the Latin for "without care." You have probably heard it said of a person, "He seems so relaxed, as if he's without a care in the world." That is the literal dictionary description of a secure person. The inner vision of "secure" reflects a sense of safety and assurance that all is well. There may be trouble on every side and storms about to strike, but deep inside there is an inner peace and tranquility because one's life is built on a solid foundation of hope for both present and future.

When one sees oneself as "secure," there results a considerable amount of emotional stability, patience, and inner confidence.

This type of self-image is not easily threatened or intimidated. The person with such an inner vision of self knows that security comes from within and not from without. He or she has learned not to put trust in money, property, status, position, or special people. Since all such externals can be lost or taken away, one's security would be gone, too. Rather, one's sense of security must come from within.

Jesus taught that the "kingdom [reign] of God is within you" (Luke 17:21). The apostle Paul explained that the Holy Spirit dwells within the believer (Rom. 8:11). What greater sense of security could one want than to know that God reigns and dwells within the heart of each of his children? If God lives within us, then does it really matter what is going on outside us? Therefore, a deep sense of inner security is available through a personal saving relationship with God through faith in Jesus Christ. (This idea will be developed in greater detail in a later chapter.)

I am reminded of how the inner eye of a hurricane is calm and peaceful, while outside a raging storm is going on. The Bible has much to say about the peace God gives to his people. This biblical concept of peace is directly related to the inner vision of "secure." Jesus said it all in these words: "Peace I leave with you; my peace I give you. I do not give to you as the world gives. Do not let your hearts be troubled and do not be afraid" (John 14:27).

People who see themselves as "secure" are not only patient and emotionally stable, but they tend to be tolerant of others who differ with them or who are different from them. They are not easily threatened by disagreements or differences of opinion. They feel free to give others the freedom to differ. As with the other labels, to see yourself as "secure" motivates you to prove it is true, in this case with calm, serene, stable, unruffled, tolerant, and understanding behavior toward others.

7. "Attractive"

You may also see yourself as "attractive," which is obviously a very positive vision of self. The "attractive" self-image moves you to be presentable, neat, orderly, outgoing, gregarious, pleasant, and even organized. What you feel on the inside about yourself is often projected on the outside. The externals often betray the nature of the internals of personality.

If you feel "attractive" on the inside, you generally want to look good on the outside. This not only affects the choice of clothes you wear and the style of your hair but also the things around you, such as the appearance of your office (even the condition of your desk?) or place of work, how your home looks, both inside and out, as well as the upkeep of the car you drive.

Whatever motivated John Wesley to teach that "cleanliness is next to godliness" must have also motivated Paul to urge his readers to let their minds dwell on "whatever is pure, whatever is lovely, whatever is admirable" (Phil. 4:8). Paul even urged slaves to behave in such a way that "they will make the teaching about God our Savior attractive" (Titus 2:10). Christians especially ought to strive to make their demeanor attractive, not unpleasant. The biblical concepts of "righteousness, peace and joy in the Holy Spirit" (Rom. 14:17) are the roots of the self-image of being "attractive," of which Paul adds that "anyone who serves Christ in this way is pleasing to God and approved by men" (v. 18). "Pleasing" and "approved" suggest "attractive." For Paul this was one way to describe the kingdom of God (v. 17). God's rule works to make us attractive both to self and to others.

8. "Cooperative"

Everyone enjoys living or working with the person who is "cooperative," which is another positive self-vision. This person is generally a joy to be around. "He is a good worker" often means that he cooperates and is easy to get along with on the job. This man sees himself as a team member, one who has learned the power of interdependence. The label "cooperative" also makes one a good family member, since one usually lives in a household with many different kinds of personalities.

The "cooperative" self-image motivates you to develop good relational skills. Such inner vision creates an awareness of the needs and characteristics of others in the circle of your interpersonal relationships. This insight provides the necessary information by which cooperation is made possible. Compromise, adjustments, and give-and-take attitudes seem natural if you see yourself as "cooperative."

The biblical goal of "peace" is closely related to being "cooperative." Jesus urged his followers to "be at peace with each other" (Mark 9:50). Paul added: "If it is possible, as far as it depends on you, live at peace with everyone" (Rom. 12:18) and similarly admonished the Corinthian Christians to learn how to cooperate with one another (1 Cor. 1:10). He also exhorted two Philippian women in conflict to "agree with each other" (Phil. 4:2). When people see themselves as agreeable, or "cooperative," they will tend to produce that kind of action. What you see is what you do.

9. "Nurturer"

One of the most needed and constructive positive labels for one's self-image is that of "nurturer." The word comes from a Latin term meaning the act of nursing. A nurturer is one who gives nourishment, who cares for another, or who furthers the development of another. Nurturing can be either physical, emotional, or psychological.

Moreover, nurturers are those who give themselves wherever or to whomever needed. Nurturing places the emphasis on giving rather than receiving, although the one nurturing always benefits from the experience. In the process of giving, nurturers tend to be expressive rather than withdrawn. They are demonstrative; that is, their behavior is marked by a display of feelings. They are inclined to display their emotions openly rather than being reserved, cool, or distant.

To view yourself as "nurturer" motivates you to encourage others. If you are such a person, you view your basic personality role as giving strength, courage, and inspiration to others. The goal of "nurturing" produced the biblical character of Barnabas. In the Book of Acts, it was Barnabas who salvaged both Saul of Tarsus and John Mark from historical obscurity by encouraging them to become what God had planned for them to be: two of the most significant leaders in the early church. Barnabas was a nickname for Joseph of Cyprus. Because of his nurturing lifestyle, the apostles renamed him Barnabas, meaning "son of encouragement" (see Acts 4:36; 9:26–27; 12:25–13:3; 15:36–41; 2 Tim. 4:11).

Jesus obviously saw himself as "nurturer," as observed in his consistent affirmation of the people around him. He freely gave himself to others, expressed his love openly and in practical ways, and was demonstrative in his compassion for needy persons. Wherever nurturers are found in homes and churches, there is much strength and stability.

10. "Happy"

The word *happy* means many different things to different people, but it continues to communicate to some degree a positive label of well-being. The word suggests good fortune, contentment, joy, gladness, being pleased, even friendliness. To see yourself as "happy" is to perceive your life as blessed and to express a light-heartedness of optimism regarding your past, present, and future.

It is often said that happiness is a choice, and I believe that is true, but it is also a perception regarding your self-image. The consequence is that if we see ourselves as "happy," then we will strive to share our happiness with others. If we perceive ourselves as "blessed," then we will want to bless the people in our circle of influence.

The Bible speaks often of happiness and joy. The Beatitudes in the Sermon on the Mount call to mind the classic passage on the subject (Matt. 5:2–12). Both Jesus and Paul talked much about joy (John 15:11; Gal. 5:22).

If you see yourself as "happy," "blessed," and "joy-filled," you are more likely to behave in a manner that brings happiness to self and others rather than communicating sadness, gloom, and depression.

11. "Realistic"

A final positive label, one which I have often observed in the positive self-image, I will describe as "realistic." So many people live in a fantasy world of unrealistic goals, dreams, and expectations that in time wear thin and produce discouragement and depression. Realism calls for seeing yourself within the limits of your own potential in the real world, rather than imagining yourself to be someone you are not nor ever will be. To perceive yourself to be "realistic" is to possess a sober vision that avoids the pretense of egotism and arrogance.

The inner vision of "realistic" values humility—the willingness to be who we are and to strive to become all that God wants us to be. It is not the absence of self-esteem, nor is it self-rejection. Humility is the highest form of self-acceptance since it does not let pride say that we must be greater and better before we can recognize our self-worth.

Humility is realism that balances our strengths with our weaknesses, our personal righteousness with our sins, our daily ups with our downs, as well as the good and the bad of each day. To see yourself as a "realistic" Christian recognizes that you are both an imperfect human being as well as a growing child of God. We are all both sinners and saints. "Realistic" perception helps us to avoid the false philosophy that dedicated and Spirit-filled Christians never have any problems. Such a viewpoint is not clear vision but foggy thinking not based on biblical realism. An inner vision of "realistic" helps us to set achievable goals for personality growth and development, and it also helps us to avoid the traps of perfectionism and fantasy. To see yourself as "realistic" helps you to keep your feet on the ground, to not be discouraged when you experience setbacks, to wait patiently on the Lord for good things to happen, and to expect growth to come, even though slowly and sometimes painfully. Positive realism is a healthy way to stay sober and sane in a world that encourages people to escape into illusions and pipe dreams.

To Sum It Up

A positive self-image is birthed and encouraged by positive label-givers. Eleven positive labels have been identified, and you may think of others. The awareness and application of these positive labels may help to provide goals for change, because a personality label implies a goal toward which one strives. These goals are our options for growth. From a biblical perspective, these are the "new clothes" Jesus Christ has given us to put on (Eph. 4:24) to wear in kingdom-of-God living.

4

The Negative Self-Image

Over the years, as I have counseled with hundreds of people who have serious problems, the one common element that stands out is that the great majority of these people have a very negative self-image. By "negative" we usually mean a poor, critical, or low evaluation of oneself. This involves a strong dislike for oneself, as evidenced by comments and attitudes of self-disparagement, belittling, criticism, and self-humiliation. People who have a negative self-image will, especially under stress, be heard to say even such remarks as "I hate myself." Such people have developed the fine art of the verbal put-down regarding themselves. These put-downs are labels that they feel they must live up to (or, in this case, live *down* to). The put-downs most often applied to oneself are "dummy," "stupid," "clumsy," "klutz," "clod," "bad," "no-good," and they are often augmented by such statements as "I can't . . ." "I'm afraid . . ." and "Nobody likes [loves] me."

People with a negative self-image can often be detected by the way they look. Their clothes (wrinkled, unclean, poorly fitted, mismatched), their weight (either extremely thin or overweight), their gait (slow, draggy, sluggish), their hair (uncombed, unkempt, extreme appearance), their posture (bent or humped over, slouchy), their facial expression (blank or bland-looking, dull, depressed, or frowning gaze), and their tone of voice (either muffled or extremely loud, mostly a low tone poorly projected and hard to understand) are all telltale signals of a low personal evaluation.

I should mention that I don't want to be unfair or unkind about the weight problem. Some people have inherited tendencies to be extremely thin or overweight. This can be a serious physical problem if rooted in their genetic makeup, early development, or even a disease process. I do not intend to be unsympathetic toward such people. Rather, I am referring in my above description to those people whose weight problem is largely due to disliking themselves intensely. A poor self-image can be the culprit behind either anorexia or an extreme overweight condition.

As with the genesis of the positive self-image, so with the negative self-image: one's background and experiences can provide a wide variety of negative labels. The person with a poor self-image has *chosen* one or several of these to wear. These labels have been provided largely by certain significant label-givers, who offer a mostly dark and distorted view of reality and life. For them, nothing is good; all is bad. They try to teach us to see the dirt on the window and thereby cause us to miss the beautiful sunset in the western evening sky.

Most people with a negative or poor self-image have adopted the derogatory labels of the negative label-givers because they believe this is the way to win their approval, love, and acceptance. The need to belong drives them to accept the dark view of life and of self. Remember that personality labels become our behavioral goals. When we label ourselves negatively, we have to "prove" the labels we have adopted are true by behaving accordingly.

Negative Label-Givers

Several negative label-givers may be identified. Together they provide a cluster of influences toward self-depreciation or self-devaluation. Early in life, as we walk through the cafeteria of identity, these influences provide us with several choices of negative labels. Most of these function in the context of the home, the school, the church, and the local community.

The primary negative label-giver is a negative family matrix. This is a family whose interpersonal relationships may be characterized as cool, distant, and somewhat impersonal. In such a family the children tend to get the idea that they are more like "things" than they are persons. The unaffectionate attitude of the parents leaves the impression that children are uninvited and unwanted guests in the home. The parents' unspoken message is: "You happened to be born, so we have to take care of you." The bottom line is: "You really aren't worth our time and attention, so stay out of sight and don't be a problem; we have more important things to do."

A negative family atmosphere may sometimes be detected by the physical appearance of the home. When the inside of the house is dark and dingy, inadequately heated in winter and cooled in summer, unkempt and messy with dirty floors and windows, and the furniture is unattractive, uncomfortable and poorly arranged, a negative atmosphere prevails for the children growing up there. When the outside of the house is cluttered with junk and trash, and the yard, trees, and shrubs are poorly kept, a negative message says to all that this family has no pride in itself. When meals are poorly prepared and unattractive, lack adequate nourishment, are sporadically served and rarely eaten together with pleasant conversation as a family, a negative message is conveyed to the children: "You are not important." When the atmosphere of the home is filled with unhappiness, criticism, and fighting, a similar negative message is sent to all: "No one is loved here because no one here is worth loving." *Unloved, unwanted,* and *worthless* spells "rejection," a heavy negative label to wear.

Another source of negative label-givers is that group of significant others who love conditionally. This kind of love is not really love; rather it is a form of limited approval or acceptance. It expresses the unspoken message that "I love you if . . ." and is communicated in various subtle ways. Where conditional love is practiced, the children and other recipients are well aware of the conditions: "I love you if you do what I tell you [. . . if you do not give me any trouble; . . . if you keep your room clean; . . . if you come in on time; . . . if you eat all the food on your plate; . . . if you go to church; . . . if you give me what I want; and so on]." The list is endless.

Conditional love means you are never really loved, never fully accepted, because no one can always live up to all the conditions perfectly. So you never really make it. You are imperfect, and therefore something is wrong with you, something is lacking. Try as hard as you may, you will fail somewhere in some way. In this case, "salvation" (love and acceptance) is by works; so there is never any assurance of your "salvation." The inevitable result is a negative self-image. Your self-worth is always conditioned upon someone else's demands. Since your self-worth is never a "given," you never really have any.

Related to conditional lovers as negative label-givers are those significant others (again, mostly parents and other close relatives) who are discouragers, critics, complainers—judges who apply faultfinding with a heavy hand. When the people who should mean the most to you are the source of consistent discouragement, it is extremely difficult to feel good about yourself. When your parents express to you more criticism than affirmation, it is natural to conclude that there is, in fact, something basically wrong with you. Likewise, constant complaining by the people whose opinions you have been taught to respect will in time wear you down to a low view of yourself. It takes a great deal of ego strength to overcome the negative effects if the significant others in your life are consistently judgmental. Most persons will not overcome such influence without strong counterbalancing sources of affirmation.

Significant others who are themselves negative personality models are perhaps the most consistent negative label-givers. Parents who have a poor self-image will in many cases rear children who will develop a poor self-image. Like produces like. If your father projects himself as a "loser" and your mother projects herself as "insecure," in time you may conclude that this is the way you should see yourself as well. If a mother models her sexuality in negative terms (e.g., sex is obnoxious and dirty), her daughter will more than likely adopt a negative view of herself as a female and view her own sexuality in the same way. Parents teach more with the force of their own self-image than they do with their words.

Related to negative modeling is negative goal-setting. When parents and older siblings set for themselves goals of failure, weakness, rejection, and fear, you are more likely to conclude that these are inevitable goals for yourself. If your parents set for themselves the goal of "not going to college" and later settled for whatever work they could find, you will be unconsciously encouraged to conclude, "I'm not college material either," which suggests, "I'm not very smart either." (This is only an illustration. Not everyone should necessarily go to college, but everyone should try to learn a trade or skill by which to earn an adequate living.)

Negative label-givers can also be institutions, such as the church. A distorted gospel preached by a negative church is often the source of negative labels for impressionable converts, rather than the Good News of the true gospel. It has been my observation that ultra-conservative churches tend to emphasize the sinful nature of the unregenerate person to the neglect of the redemptive status of the born-again disciple of Christ. Raise this point among those with a fundamentalist mind-set and watch their reaction, and you will see what I mean. And they will quote the "appropriate" verses from the Bible to make their countering point. For example: "There is no one righteous, not even one. . . .there is no one who does good, not even one" (Rom. 3:10, 12). Such passages are easily quoted out of context.

Such negative doom-sayers seem to ignore Romans 8:1–2: "Therefore, there is now no condemnation for those who are in Christ Jesus, because through Christ Jesus the law of the Spirit of life set me free from the law of sin and death," as well as 2 Corinthians 5:17: "Therefore, if anyone is in Christ, he is a new creation; the old has gone, the new has come!"

If, during your early formative years, you attend a church where you hear over and over again, "You are really a very bad person, because God says so," the weight of such religious authority is bound to make a negative impression. The tragedy of this is that even becoming a child of God seems to make no basic difference in the conclusion of such a negative philosophy of life. You will still consider yourself a "bad person," still a "sinner," although saved by grace. Yet, when you read the Bible, it is revealing that the Christian is referred to more as a "saint" than as a "sinner."

However, the nay-sayers ignore these facts which are in the same Bible they claim to believe as the inerrant Word of God. This seems to be a belief in selected inspiration, that is, the "spot theory" of revelation. Only the "bad person" spots are considered inspired; the "redeemed person" portions are conveniently ignored. No wonder that such negative affronts to the believer's self-esteem turn away many thinking people from such churches. Of course, they do attract those who already have negative self-images, those whose poor self-esteem is "confirmed" by so-called religious authority!

Closely related to this source of negative labeling are those significant persons (parents, pastors, Bible-school teachers) who have a distorted theology that centers on a strictly punitive God. Their view of the God and Father of our Lord Jesus Christ has been twisted into a concept of an extremely punitive deity. "God is love" (1 John 4:8) has been functionally translated into "God is angry, and mostly at you because you are a bad person." Now, most assuredly, the Bible teaches the wrath and judgment of God regarding unbelief and the rebellion of a sinful nature (see Rom. 1:18—3:20). But the Bible also teaches that the God of love has thoroughly and adequately dealt with man's sin problem through the death and resurrection of his Son, Jesus Christ, and that through faith in him, we are forgiven and become new persons in Christ (see Rom. 3:21—6:23). Yet this other half of God's revealed Word is blindly overlooked by so many who continue to wallow in their own negative self-image and teach others to do likewise.

Even some of our hymns reflect the distorted theology of a punitive God who relishes in putting his people down. I once came across an old hymn written in the nineteenth century that has this line in it: "Oh, to be nothing!" Can you imagine anyone who has read the Scriptures regarding the believer's new position in Christ exulting in being "nothing" for Jesus? This is simply the result of biblical ignorance, perpetuated negative self-vision, and low self-esteem. To suggest that God enjoys and blesses such low evaluation of self is biblically appalling. I have observed through the years that some people who teach this kind of theology are extremely arrogant and egotistical, inconsistent though it seems. About such spiritual pride, the Bible does have something to say (see Prov. 8:13; 16:18; 1 John 2:16)!

It is sad and tragic that so many gullible children and unsuspecting adults are influenced by such negative label-givers. The next obvious question is: What are the major negative labels that people may attach to themselves? Eleven will be suggested. There may be others.

Negative Labels

Negative labels are what I call "personality syndromes." A syndrome may be defined as "a group of signs and symptoms that occur together and characterize a particular abnormality," or (in a more medical context) as "an aggregate or set of concurrent symptoms indicating the presence and nature of a disease." From these definitions I suggest that a personality syndrome is a cluster of negative self-perceptions that create a variety of behavioral problems related to one's interpersonal relationships. This means that a negative self-image is the product of adopting for oneself one or more personality labels that reflect a negative vision of oneself and the surrounding world.

One label or trait usually tends to stand out over the others, yet each one both feeds upon and encourages the others. Therefore, a cluster of negative labels works together to produce a certain degree of personality disintegration. I am reminded here of Paul's reference to the "works of the flesh" (Gal. 5:19–21), where the plural *works* (compare with the singular *fruit of the Spirit* in Gal. 5:22) suggests disunity or disintegration. This will become quite obvious as we discuss the following negative labels.

1. "Rejected"

Unwanted children will more than likely take on this label quite early in life. Someday we may be able to prove that a child can even pick up prenatal messages of rejection from a mother who does not want the child. When my mother became pregnant with me in 1931, the dark days of the Depression were under way. She already had two children. The last thing a woman needed during those economically hard times was another baby. From comments my mother made to my wife years later, I suspect that she did not really want a third child. This did not mean that my mother did not love me after I was born, but for nine months she may have been sending messages of rejection to the fetus in her body. In my early childhood, somewhere between ages two and three, my mother went away for what seemed like a very long time to have a hysterectomy. I don't recall the details, but I do remember feeling confusion regarding why my mother had left me. I felt she had rejected me. This was on a feeling level. Looking back, I now realize that there was no truth in what I felt. But, as a child, feeling it made it so.

The rejection syndrome includes feelings of worthlessness and unlovableness. To feel "rejected" implies that you are of little or no worth. Persons who have value and who therefore are loved are not generally discarded as unwanted. When such rejection is experienced, a poor self-image inevitably results.

Then a snowball effect takes place. What you see is what you do. If you perceive yourself as rejectable, you have to prove that such vision is correct. Subtly and subconsciously you set yourself up to be rejected time and again by doing and saying things that will turn off the people you live and work with. The rejection syndrome is often the dynamic behind divorce-prone people, behind employees who get themselves fired from one job after another, and behind individuals who seemingly "can't get along with anyone."

Furthermore, the person who wears the "rejected" label will be inclined to read rejection into most everything said or done about him or her. Facial expressions, tone of voice, even an apparent compliment, may be interpreted as rejection if you envision yourself as rejectable. It doesn't matter whether or not the rejection is real. Feeling it makes it so.

2. "Loser"

The label I see most often among the people I have counseled through the years is that of "loser." This is the person who feels that he or she can't do anything right. Being labeled a "loser" results in feelings of incompetence, inadequacy, and inferiority. This person was probably told as a child in a thousand and one ways: "You are not able to do that; you are inadequate; you lack the necessary skills; you are stupid and no-good." He or she believed it and bought it. The label stuck.

In analyzing early memories, I have observed that losers tend to remember events or experiences involving some kind of falling or stumbling. Such memories serve to reflect and even reinforce the loser syndrome.

Losers have to "prove" they are, in fact, a bad investment. What better way can one prove he or she is a loser than to lose one's marriage? Or by getting oneself fired from one job after another due to incompetency? I have known certain pastors with a persecution complex who always tend to be the focus of conflict in the churches they serve, resulting in their eventual dismissal. Strange as it sounds, such people need to lose in order to feel "happy." This sick kind of "happiness" is merely a confirmation of the way losers see themselves.

American society is replete with classic examples of "losers": prison inmates, alcoholics, drug addicts, divorce-prone people, school dropouts, the chronically unemployed, and people with certain chronic psychosomatic illnesses. Obviously, not everyone in these categories could necessarily be classified a "loser." There are often extenuating circumstances, such as in the case of Lenel Geter, the young black engineer from Greenville, Texas. In 1983 he was wrongly convicted of a crime he did not commit and spent eighteen months in prison before being released after new evidence and a subsequent confession by the real criminal proved Geter's innocence. Some people become hooked on drugs accidentally, and some youths are forced out of school due to family financial circumstances. But most people in these situations are there because it "proves" they are losers. Their low vision of self moves them in the direction of loser-type behavior.

3. "Insecure"

The "insecure" label is almost as prevalent as is "loser." It is basically rooted in fear. At first, it seems that to see oneself as "insecure" reveals more about how a person sees the world and life than it does about that person's self-vision. Of course, to the insecure, life itself is a threatening situation and the world is a dangerous place. However, insecurity involves a deep inner self-perception. It is a way of saying, "I really can't cope with all that is stacked against me. I cannot face up to the kind of world we live in. I am a fear-filled person when I think of what is expected of me. I see myself as lacking the necessary qualities for facing the challenges and uncertainties of the present and future."

The "insecure" syndrome tends to paralyze or immobilize a person so far as performing even the normal responsibilities of life generally expected of that person's age level. The insecure one is, more often than not, a withdrawn person: shy, retreating, overly quiet (with one possible exception), socially inactive, unaffectionate, unwilling to compete with others, something of a loner. The one possible exception, previously mentioned, is the excessively macho person: the loud, braggadocio type who is full of pretension and cockiness but actually feels very insecure and is trying to cover up a fearful inner self. Often I have found that underneath the noise of the braggart is a little boy who is running scared. Macho language and behavior is very likely an over-compensation for deep feelings of insecurity. I am reminded of the sermon outline left on the pulpit one Sunday. The custodian noticed the preacher had written in the margin of his third point the words: "Weak point, shout here."

The insecure person tends to believe that security comes from without rather than from within. That is, security is thought to be rooted in one's job, money, property, possessions, certain people (parents, a husband, a wife, one's children), or social status. Yet these things can be taken away or lost. Then what can one do? It is hard for the "insecure" to understand that security must come from down deep in the inner recesses of one's being.

If you see yourself as "insecure," then you have to prove the label is true, and your behavior will be motivated by fear. You will be like the person Jesus talked about who buried his talent out of fear and did nothing productive with it (Matt. 25:14–30). He "proved" his insecurity by wasting his abilities. He lost what he had, the very thing he was afraid of. An "insecure" self-image is yet another example of a self-fulfilling prophecy. "Insecure" people create an insecure world for themselves.

4. "Repulsive"

Another negative personality label is the vision of oneself as "repulsive." This label takes one of two possible directions: ugly or dirty. The first has to do with looks or appearance. In a beauty-saturated culture, an "ugly" self-image can be devastatingly negative. When one sees oneself as physically unattractive, even hideous, feelings of repulsion emerge.

Since the nature of one's looks are subjectively defined, the facts do not always support the conclusion. Remember Peggy in chapter 2? She is a very beautiful young woman who for years considered herself "ugly." Most any red-blooded American male would consider her extremely attractive. But because she is 4 feet 9 inches in height, she had looked upon herself as "an ugly runt." All of her other features were self-defined in light of her one "abnormality" (as she saw it). In time she has gradually begun to accept herself as "petite," a more positive way of perceiving her size. However, for years (especially through her teens and twenties) she had seen herself as physically ugly and therefore repulsive to others and herself.

The other direction the "repulsive" label may take is that of "dirty," which carries a strong moral connotation. Sexual hangups tend to prevail here. People who learn to envision themselves as "dirty" were usually convinced early in life that their body and its functions were a moral handicap. Poor potty training may have contributed to conveying such a label. Often the person's mother felt negative toward her own body and all bodily functions, especially the body's sexuality. By communicating that the human body is "evil" in some way, such parents can pass on the deepseated belief that one's body is "dirty," as is connected with its normal functioning. Since humans are body-oriented creatures, it is very easy for the "dirty" label to cover the entire personality.

If you would like to test whether, or to what degree, you wear this particular negative label, go into your bathroom or some other room that has a full-length mirror. By yourself, take off all your clothes and look at yourself in the mirror. Take a pencil and pad and write down what you feel. You don't have to look like Miss America or Charles Atlas to feel good about your body. You may be a little overweight (most American adults are) or a little too thin. But, overall, how do you feel about the way you look? If what you write down conveys "repulsive" feelings, you may be wearing this label to some degree. To move toward a more positive self-image, it may help to remember that the body of the Christian is defined as a "temple of the Holy Spirit" (1 Cor. 6:19). Now, looking in the mirror, what do you see? A temple of the Holy Spirit is never "ugly" or "dirty."

If what you see is what you do, it is only natural for the "repulsive" self-vision to prove its accuracy by "dirty" and/or "ugly" behavior. If you see yourself as "repulsive," there will be a strong motivation to behave in such a way as to cause others to be repelled by you.

5. "Weak"

Often observed among my counselees is the label "weak," worn by someone who sees him or herself as a victim of life's circumstances. This person cannot cope or deal successfully with the hard knocks of life. "Weak" may also translate into "sickly," especially if such a person has learned early in life that special attention is given when one is ill. So sickliness and weakness become the routes to attention or special recognition by means of nurture and comfort.

I remember a young mother who had been the oldest child in her family. However, her younger brother had "dethroned" her from her favored position as the oldest. He was especially his father's favorite child. But his older sister soon learned that when she was ill, her parents' attention turned to her, and she became the favored one again. In that sense, "weak" for her spelled "strength." However, the "weak" label backfired for her as an adult, married, with children of her own. Her husband and children became gradually disenchanted with her when they would come home from work and school to find her usually "sick" in bed—with no supper prepared, no clean house, and no demonstrative romance for hubby. Her "illness" was mostly asthmatic, with obvious psychosomatic roots. What brought her nurturing attention as a child was bringing her serious relational problems as an adult. Although her daily behavior was proving that her self-image as "weak" was true, it was also destroying her marriage and home.

The inner vision of self as "weak" also produces an overly dependent person. If you perceive your self as physically, emotionally, mentally, or relationally "crippled," other people are needed as "crutches." In most relationships, this can become quite burdensome after a while. The dependency is in time perceived by others as self-chosen and unnecessary and may be considered irresponsibility by a person's loved ones and friends. Relationships in these circumstances can become strained and fragile.

Evangelical Christians have learned from Scripture that genuine weakness and authentic limitations can become the means for discovering the power of God in one's life. Paul learned that offering his physical weaknesses to Christ brought unusual power for living. He concluded, "For when I am weak, then I am strong" (2 Cor. 12:10). But to use "weakness" as an excuse for attention-getting and as a cover for irresponsibility would for Paul be totally objectionable in a Christian.

6. "Angry"

Anger is probably the most powerful emotion in the human reservoir of feelings. There are different theories that describe what causes anger to erupt. Three are significantly close to the truth, in my judgment. One is the punitive theory: "I will punish you with my anger." Another is the defense theory: "I will protect myself from a threatening situation with my anger." A third is the justice theory: "I will use my anger to change an unjust situation into one in which justice and fairness prevail." Anger is a normal human emotion that I believe God gave each of us to use in constructive ways. However, anger out of control can be very destructive to life, property, and self. It can also destroy relationships: a marriage, a family, or friendships.

This is where the negative "angry" label comes in. When a person chooses to see him or herself as consistently and justifiably "angry," life takes on for that person a combative and hostile vision. Both self and others are perceived in terms of anger. This person carries a "mad" around all the time. Feeling threatened, abused, or blocked from achieving certain goals, this person regularly expresses some form of hostility, either directly (shouts, hits, or even kills) or indirectly (pouts, withholds something wanted or needed by others, withdraws, gets ulcers, or becomes chronically depressed).

The person with an "angry" self-image has one basic style of behavior: attack, attack, attack. Whether the subconscious rationale is to punish, to defend, or to change, if anger becomes one's dominating perception of self and life, someone may end up getting hurt. That someone usually ends up being several someones. To prevent serious damage from being done, certain questions need to be considered. Who is in control? What direction will the anger take? What goals will guide its use? Is there sufficient inner strength to keep one's anger within constructive limits?

But as long as one's basic self-vision is "angry," there will be real problems in one's interpersonal relationships because most people eventually become weary of someone who always wants to dump mad behavior on them, however justified that person feels in doing so. The "angry" self usually becomes a very lonely person because his or her steady venting of anger has an isolating effect from others. The angry vision produces an angry world full of alienated people.

7. *"Judgmental"*

Another negative personality label is "judgmental," the self-image of a perfectionistic person. This vision of self and the world around is that nothing is right, something is always wrong, out-of-place, and unacceptable. A friend of mine is a perfectionistic housekeeper who sweeps every room of the house every day. Every speck of dirt must go and can never be tolerated. Another friend of mine is a perfectionistic parent. Her children have always had to be perfect models to be displayed in public to prove that she is the perfect mother. All through the years the family has simply tolerated her judgmental evaluation of their behavior. There has always been enough love mixed in that they have been willing to overlook her criticisms, at least most of the time.

Perfectionism is usually both the result and expression of conditional love. The way to rear a perfectionistic child is to come across in thousands of ways over the years with messages of "I love you if . . . ." Of course, no child can live up to the usually unrealistic standards set forth with that kind of love, because no child is perfect. A conditionally loved child never feels thoroughly loved, because he or she can never reach the standard. "I love you if you stay clean." What child can stay clean all day? There is always a failure, a flaw, a fault to point out, to work on, to remove. This judgmental atmosphere will produce children who are nervous wrecks. Never having felt thoroughly loved, they have a very hard time loving others.

The "judgmental" self-image makes one hard to live with, causes one to see the world as an evil place, and even to see morally neutral or good things as bad in themselves (for example, sex is dirty, affection is smothering, money is tainted, church is full of hypocrites, politics are corrupt, the human body is ugly). "Judgmental" people are probably hardest on themselves. Consequently, they almost never reach self-esteem because they can never feel good about their imperfect selves. Attempts at self-love always fall short since there are always flaws to point out in oneself. The conditional love of the parents is repeated in the child's self-image. For perfectionists there can be neither self-love nor love for the imperfect people around them.

The critical spirit of the "judgmental" self-vision has the same effect as the "angry" label: isolation and loneliness. Who wants a steady diet of complaints, criticism, and judgment?

8. "Irresponsible"

When a person sees himself as "irresponsible," he is not likely to think of himself in terms of irresponsibility. No one word exactly describes this particular label, or vision of self. However, one statement might sum it up: "When I see myself, I see a person who doesn't really care what others think or whether or not the expectations of others are lived up to. I care even less whether I fulfill the responsibilities of my role obligations." Such an inner vision results in what might be called an "irresponsible" lifestyle.

This self-image is obviously a very selfish one, but its roots are much deeper than mere self-centeredness. At the roots are a lack of self-confidence, immaturity, low motivation, the absence of a meaning and purpose for life, maybe even a heavy dose of anger and resentment, or possibly an overwhelming sense of discouragement. The roots of irresponsibility are as complex as human personality itself. However, some would argue biblically that irresponsibility is the very root of sin itself, as depicted in the story of Adam and Eve. Those first two humans refused to take responsibility for what God had given them and had told them. They "copped out" at every turn in their primary responsibility to God.

The inner vision of "irresponsible" may express itself in laziness or lack of motivation to do anything constructive. It may also be revealed in uncooperative behavior, going one's own way, refusing to work with or get along with others. One who is often discouraged may be living out an "irresponsible" self-vision, feeling that attempts to be a responsible person in the past did not work (or pay off, or succeed, or whatever)—"Why keep trying? It isn't worth the effort." The "irresponsible" label of self may also express itself in a rebellious lifestyle: "getting even with the establishment" (whether the government or one's parents or God and the church). For an example, recall the "irresponsible" hippies of the 1960s, protesting against various established forms of authority.

Of course, as with all labels, what you see is what you do. If you see yourself as "irresponsible," you will prove that you are, in one way or another, and everyone else "can go jump in the lake."

9. "Boss"

Another negative label I see a lot is closely related to the "insecure" label: "boss." To see yourself as "boss" means that you feel compelled to dominate everyone and everything around you. I believe that this is an expression of insecurity. In testing and analyzing counselees who seek to dominate others, I have found that deep inside them is a strong feeling of insecurity and fear. They feel driven to be "in charge" lest their world fall apart.

I have sometimes found the "boss" self-image among wives and mothers who were the oldest in their family of origin and now feel compelled to dominate their husbands and children. Mother is a "Queen Elizabeth" and father is only a "Prince Philip." This woman is driven to be in control of everything related to the home lest the family situation collapse. She tends to stifle every desire for freedom by the other family members and fears that if she loses control, she will lose everything. Mother-as-boss usually fails to see that the main reason she has come for counseling is that she is about to lose everything in her marriage and family because of her strict dominating pattern of behavior.

However, I have also counseled many men who are doing the same thing. Their male-chauvinist or macho image motivates them to "show the little woman and the kids who's boss." A growing number of women in recent years are becoming deeply resentful of being ordered around like slaves by their husbands. Such men come for counseling only after being threatened with divorce by an angry wife who is fed up with being treated like a thing rather than a person with feelings, needs, and abilities of her own.

The label of "boss" is worn by the insecure person who feels that control, domination, and power are necessary to achieve any self-worth. If you are not "boss," you are a nobody! Marriage-and-family counseling often exposes power struggles between spouses and between parents and children. Such unhappy people can be helped if they can discover a more Christian approach to family relationships. In marriage and in parenting, why not loving servanthood for both parties, rather than dominance by one and submission by the other? Jesus was dealing with the "boss" syndrome in Matthew 20:25–28. (More on this later.)

10. "V.I.P."

The "V.I.P." label simply stands for "Very Important Person." I have seen this worn most often by an only child. I consider this a negative label because, more often than not, it creates a lot of problems for the bearer, especially in one's marriage and family life. The only child tends to have this self-vision because during the early formative years he or she was the recipient of most of the parents' time and attention. Since there is no sibling competition, the only child usually gets lots of attention and grows up expecting it. Of course, not all only children choose to wear the "V.I.P." label.

Whether or not one who wears this label was an only child, he or she needs lots of attention and recognition in order to feel any worth. This person tends to be extremely self-centered and prone to take rather than give. Without sufficient attention and recognition, this person will be very unhappy and will find ways to let others know it. He or she will seek attention at any price, even at cost of a marriage or a close friendship.

People who see themselves as a "V.I.P." may, in a few cases, even go so far as to have what might be called a child-of-destiny syndrome. Some parents have raised a child who shows exceptional talents (real or imaginary) to believe that he or she was destined by God or fate to become a sort of messianic leader or super-hero. There are certain authoritarian personalities who are classic examples of this pathological personality syndrome. When such children become political or religious leaders, they feel destined to rule with a determined hand and, if blocked from doing so, will seek to ruin what they cannot rule. (Fortunately for the rest of the world, many a "V.I.P." is programmed to self-destruct.)

These can be very dangerous people. Some have been known to split churches or denominations by insisting on having their way. Others have led nations into war in order to purge the world of "evil," as they define it. They may become so determined to be known and followed that they can epitomize evil at its worst. (Read M. Scott Peck, *The People of the Lie* [New York: Simon and Schuster, 1983] for an insightful treatment of evil people hiding under the umbrella of religion.) Certainly not all "V.I.P." people are evil, but they can become vulnerable to some extreme forms of pathological behavior.

An inner vision of "V.I.P." reveals a terrible lack of the meaning of humility. It rarely occurs to such people that they need to learn how to stroke and recognize themselves. Unless they learn that their sense of self-worth must come from within rather than from others, they will always experience stress and frustration over not receiving "enough" attention.

11. "Pious"

The last negative label I will identify is "pious." This is no re-
pudiation of sincere and deeply felt religious devotion. One dictionary definition of the word *pious* is "behavior marked by conspicuous religiosity or self-conscious virtue." The major trait
found in this personality label is false humility. Since I have observed this more in religious people, I choose the term *pious* to
describe it. This is a type of spiritual pride, projecting oneself to
be super-religious or virtuous by acting humble, spiritual, self-
negating, submissive, meek, lowly, apologetic, retreating. This is
the extreme opposite of the "V.I.P." syndrome. The main problem
here is that such people want everyone to know that they are this
way.

Such exaggerated piosity is a type of humility, but it is based on
low self-esteem. It is tragic that some people have been taught that
to be truly religious or spiritual they must constantly put themselves down and avoid self-esteem, which they consider a sinful
expression of man's carnal nature. For these folk, a positive self-
image is a result of sinful pride rather than God's transforming
grace.

But, if you see yourself as "pious" in the sense of false humility
(low self-esteem), you will prove the label is true by a show of false
religiosity that generally turns most people off. It is most unfortunate that Christianity has sometimes been given a bad reputation by people with a "pious" inner vision who parade their
poor self-esteem as the height of Christian faith.

To Sum It Up

Awareness of negative labels provides us targets to aim at for
exposing the roots of our behavioral problems in interpersonal relationships. From a Christian perspective, these are the "old
clothes" to be cast off. These are behavioral goals to be rejected
and replaced with "new self" goals. Then we no longer need these
negative labels to win love, approval, and acceptance.

In Christ, the Christian has already been loved, approved, and
accepted. In Christ, new and positive personality labels are available. These become the new goals for the transformation of one's
behavior, attitudes, and feelings by the power of the Holy Spirit.

_____ 5 ___

The Pain of the
Negative Self-Image

When Gregg entered my office I could tell immediately that something was wrong. His facial expression revealed a deep inner pain. His wife, Sarah, had just left him. It was their third separation in only five years of marriage. This time Gregg knew it would be final. She was never coming back. He said that he actually felt a sense of relief, yet the pain was real and would not go away.

Gregg's life story was one of rejection in what seemed a thousand different experiences. He was an unwanted child at birth. During his early formative years, he felt unloved and worthless. His father was always too busy to spend much time with him. His mother had four other children to raise, and a fifth child was "the last straw." It seemed that no one in the family ever fully accepted him as a meaningful part of the scene.

It didn't take long for me to see that the primary label hanging around Gregg's neck read "rejected." And it hurt! Each experience of rejection brought additional pain, and he couldn't stand it any longer. He came crying for help, for some kind of psychological or spiritual anesthesia.

Such self-image labels as "rejected," "loser," "insecure," and "repulsive" are negative because they function primarily to destroy interpersonal relationships and make it virtually impossible to achieve any appreciable degree of self-esteem. The very absence of self-esteem results in emotional and relational pain. Moreover, the various relational problems that negative personality labels tend to bring about can yield additional pain: the trauma of divorce, the loss of a job, rejection by a "friend," fear of the unknown in reaching out to potential friends and new challenges, the loss of respect from significant others, anxiety over one's acceptability, frustration over unachieved vocational or social goals.

The power of the psychological label is awesome. The labels we wear identify the nature of the self. This is who we are. We may be *homo sapiens*, but the kind of human beings we are is determined by "the set of our sails," the labels we wear. If the labels we wear are predominantly negative, a poor self-image results, which brings psychological pain of one degree or another. But what exactly causes the pain?

Compulsion to Prove the Labels Are True

Whether one has a positive or a negative self-image, a human being possesses a deep and strong inner compulsion to "prove" that the personality labels being worn are indeed true. For example, if I see myself as "boss," I must prove that my perception is true by controlling everyone around me. Harry Crenshaw was clearly the "boss" at both home and work. He treated his wife, Alice, as "the little woman." His three children were the family serfs to do as he commanded. No one was supposed to ever question Harry's word. He managed his fast-food drive-in the same way, barking orders to all the employees throughout the day. This was Harry's way of proving reality as he saw it. Any other pattern of behavior would have seemed unnatural to him. To change his way of treating others would be like trying to convince him that the sun rose each morning in the west. To be Harry meant to be "boss."

Yet, inside, Harry was miserable. He had no friends. His wife deeply resented his demands. His children considered him distant and unloving. It was difficult for Harry to understand that to be "boss" also meant to experience the pain of loneliness and isolation. He found out through the years that it is very lonely at the top, and that can hurt.

Yet, ironically, the compulsion to prove that one's personality label is true is the way to maintain one's "sanity." What you see in yourself has to be "correct" or confusion will result. That is, your view of reality will be too anxiety-ridden to maintain emotional balance if you can't trust your own perception. But if your inner vision results in the wearing of negative labels, some kind of emotional and relational pain will result. Harry's domination drove his family members and his employees to dislike him. And, for most people, to be disliked by those closest to you can be extremely painful.

This inner compulsion to prove the labels are true is also a way to gain the approval of one's label-givers. In early childhood, Harry's father, a frustrated veteran army officer, had convinced Harry that the way to achieve security and worth was to dominate those around him. Harry desperately wanted the approval of his often-absent father. By adopting the label of "boss" from his father's expectations, Harry sought to win Dad's love. However, now as a father, husband, and employer the dominating vision of himself was backfiring in his interpersonal relationships. Even though he had won the approval of his father, he lost the acceptance of others in his life who were now more important to him than his father ever was. He paid a very painful price for his vision of self as "boss." The same point could be illustrated with other negative labels. Negative labels tend to be destructive of meaningful relationships.

We Prove the Labels Are True by Our Behavior

The truth of the labels found in a negative self-image is a matter of definition and perception. Whatever the facts are, we have to prove that the labels we wear are correct, and we do this by our behavior. Remember that (as Adler taught us) all behavior is goal-oriented. Our personality labels are the goals toward which our behavior strives.

Betty Dickson was a beautiful sixteen-year-old high-school sophomore who was driving her parents up the wall with her rowdy behavior, insulting language, and low grades at school. Her parents had adopted her at sixteen months of age. Betty perceived her first months of life as a time of severe rejection. Unwanted by her biological mother, who was an unmarried teenager, and then passed around between three sets of paid foster parents before finally being adopted, there never seemed to be any deep emotional bonding to permanent parents during her first months of life. There remained a deep fear that she would eventually be rejected again and passed on to other strangers. Consequently, Betty perceived herself to be "insecure" and was driven by fear of an uncertain future.

Betty's "insecure" and "rejected" self-image served as the dominant goals of her actions, which caused her adoptive parents to respond with tighter controls and angry feelings, which in turn fed her feelings of insecurity. If she kept up this kind of behavior, they would probably "kick her out of the house," she reasoned. This would prove that her "insecure" and "rejected" labels were true.

Negative personality labels are like heavy neck-chains that weigh us down. They control our actions, which cause all kinds of problems in our relationships with others. Proving the truth of these labels starts with a general feeling of low self-esteem. If you perceive yourself to be rejected (or a loser, insecure, repulsive, weak, angry, critical, irresponsible, and so on), you are not very likely to feel good about yourself.

Low self-esteem is emotionally painful. It hurts to see yourself unloved, unwanted, worthless, scared, lazy, losing, weak, helpless, ugly, dirty, unrecognized, or whatever. It would be less painful to take a one-time physical beating. Low self-esteem is continual and is spelled m-i-s-e-r-y.

Yet these bad feelings are followed by bad actions, since the feelings need the confirmation of behavior. Negative labels tend to produce destructive, defeating, demeaning behavior patterns. Betty's "insecure" vision of self spawned her rowdiness, profanity, temper, anger, and low grades in school. As might be expected, this created situations at home and school that confirmed to her that her life was very uncertain, that she might be rejected and passed on to others once again. Her destructive and defeating behavior was proving that she was indeed "insecure." Had she not come for counseling, she would probably have gotten into further trouble, such as failing her courses, being suspended from school, becoming pregnant as an unwed teenager, being arrested on drug charges, traffic violations, or stealing, or becoming a runaway from home. When Betty changed her primary label to "secure," she changed her behavior to constructive expressions.

Personal Frustrations

This chapter could have been titled "How to Be Miserable." A person with a negative self-image "needs" to feel miserable, since this is his or her reality. Such a person can be "happy" only when feeling miserable. Possessing a negative self-image is a type of psychological and emotional masochism, whereby one enjoys self-inflicted pain. The sure way to misery is through one's inner vision of self as worthless, unloved, weak, repulsive, insecure, bad, unwanted, and so on.

The emotional pain felt by persons with a poor self-image tends to be experienced in a variety of frustrations regarding reversals and disappointments in interpersonal relationships of one sort or another. The "loser" syndrome illustrates this fact vividly. Of all the negative self-images I deal with in counseling, this is the one confronted most often. Nothing is quite so frustrating as losing at whatever task one seeks to carry out. No reasonable person really desires to lose or to fail.

One minister I counseled for several months was losing at every turn in his life. Roger Carter's modest church was becoming smaller each month, and in a city of over 100,000 this situation could not be blamed on a lack of people. While other churches in his community were growing, his was shrinking. The monthly report to his denominational superiors was a regular reminder of his vocational failure. His schoolteacher wife, Carolyn, was very dissatisfied with their marriage, so Roger was losing at home, too. Carolyn needed to get to bed by 10:00 P.M. in order to get enough sleep to rise early for a full day at school. But Roger chose to be a night owl and rarely went to bed before 2:00 A.M. Needless to say, their sex life was a flop, another "proof" of failure for Roger. Roger's bluntness with his official board brought negative responses from his church leaders, further evidence of his failure as a person.

When Roger and Carolyn came for counseling, Roger was obviously a painfully frustrated man. On the surface he did not want to lose, yet he was losing. He was living out his self-image script as "loser." Roger put off seeking help for a long time, since it was very difficult for this minister to admit that he had a personal problem he could not handle himself. Yes, it was even painful to come for counseling, but Roger's self was in bondage to a deeply rooted negative self-image, and he did not know how to break free.

The "rejected" syndrome is a bondage of worthlessness and unlovableness. It is a prison of pain to feel unwanted. It hurts when you feel you do not have a meaningful place in a significant cluster of relationships.

The "insecure" syndrome is a bondage of fear that paralyzes and prevents you from seeking close friends and rewarding achievements. It hurts when you are afraid of your present and future.

The "repulsive" syndrome is a bondage of self-depreciation and false guilt, usually based on faulty information and distorted evaluation or interpretation. A feeling of ugliness or a sense of moral guilt can be deeply painful.

The "weak" syndrome is a bondage of helplessness, debilitating dependence, and, in some cases, crippling psychosomatic sickliness. It is painful to know that people are looking to you for strength and you are offering them only weakness, especially since you don't know what to do about it.

The "angry" syndrome is a bondage of hostility, antagonism, and a feeling of being threatened. It is misery striking back. It is fear out of control, seeking to protect yourself from real or imaginary enemies. Anger gone wild not only hurts emotionally but can do great damage to one's body. Some physical pain is often the result of the barbs of anger hooking one's flesh. Those who carry around a "mad" all the time are truly hurting themselves deeply.

The "judgmental" syndrome is a bondage of legalistic moral perfectionism, wherein nothing is ever right and many things are always wrong, out-of-place, or unacceptable. You can imagine how miserable were the people who could even find fault with Jesus! This is the bondage of having been conditionally loved as children. They were never truly loved, and it is very painful not to have ever felt lovable.

The "irresponsible" syndrome is a bondage of immaturity, sluggishness, laziness, selfishness, rebelliousness, and eventually discouragement. It is the pain of the drones, who fail not only others but themselves as well.

The "boss" syndrome is a bondage of power that lacks respect for others, in that relationships are viewed as a means to one's own ends rather than ends in themselves. The compulsion to dominate is also a bondage of fear that unless one rules over others, one's little world will come apart at the seams. This is the pain of loneliness at the domination pinnacle, where control is mistaken for leadership.

The "V.I.P." syndrome is a bondage of attention-seeking and craving for recognition, of which there is never enough. It is the lonely existence of self-centeredness, the pain of egotism and arrogance. As others grow weary of one's expectations, there comes an emotional narcissism that hurts.

The "pious" syndrome is a bondage of false humility, spiritual pride, and hypocrisy. It is painful to know that while on the surface you are projecting some kind of virtue, deep inside you know it is not genuine. Hypocrisy is always painful, whether or not the hypocrisy is admitted.

Interpersonal Conflicts in Relationships

It is clear to see how the personality labels worn by a person with a negative self-image result in all sorts of interpersonal conflicts. Each negative label offers a script for a drama of painful relationships.

The "rejected" label sets in motion behavior patterns that actually cause one to be rejected by others. Bobby Stinson's poor self-image bore such a label. No one loved or liked him, according to Bobby. He had felt this way as far back as he could remember. Though he was intelligent, capable, and effective as an engineer at an energy-research laboratory, he couldn't seem to get along with his co-workers. When asked what the problem was, Bobby simply responded, "They just don't like me. We have nothing in common except our work, and everyone at work avoids me during coffee breaks and at lunch time. Some say I'm impossible to work with."

When a fellow worker was asked about Bobby's relationships at work, he replied, "Bobby's imagining that no one likes him. He is a bit reserved, and there are times when he can lose his temper when things don't go to suit him. But Bobby's not very friendly himself; he has no sense of humor and doesn't seem to be open to friendly conversation during breaks. If he feels rejected, it's his own fault. Believe me, we've all tried to reach out to him, but he seems to carry a chip on his shoulder."

Bobby was setting himself up to be rejected because inside himself he saw a person who was worthless, unlovable, and unwanted. Slide rules and computers he could work with quite well, but when it came to people it was another story. His inner vision made certain he was a victim. Rejection within precipitated rejection without. And rejection always hurts.

Likewise, the "loser" label sets in motion behavior patterns that bring to pass losing experiences. I have seen this most often in marital conflicts. Charlene Jones was an attractive and intelligent mother of two children and the wife of the manager of a major department store. She saw herself to be a "loser" in various ways, but particularly in human relationships. Charlene's husband, Dawson, complained that his wife constantly put herself down with comments about her own "stupidity," "inferiority," and "incompetence." She felt she could never do anything exactly right.

Dawson noticed that Charlene, under stress would say something like, "I know that I'm just not a good wife. You deserve a better woman than I am." To make things worse, she seemed to set herself up to fail: sexually by a lack of response; financially by overspending and carelessly failing to keep the checkbook stubs up-to-date; in matters of spousal affection by stubbornly refusing to take any initiative to hug or kiss her husband; in disciplining the children by always deferring to Dawson to take care of such matters after he came home from work; and even in housekeeping by an almost total lack of organization and neatness. In time, Dawson's nerves wore thin. Charlene seemed to be doing everything to prove that she was a loser in her marriage.

The final straw came when Dawson found out that his wife had begun secretly drinking at home during the day. As alcohol became a symbolic indicator of her loser status, Charlene's pain was almost unbearable. Had Dawson not brought her to counseling, Charlene would probably have ended up both an alcoholic and a divorcée.

Similarly, the "insecure" label creates an insecure world for the bearer. An inner vision of insecurity will define close personal relationships as threatening and fearful. Aubrey Simpson was a big man physically. A farmer and truck mechanic, he was also a bi-vocational pastor of a small rural church. He and his wife, Pam, had four sons. Although Pam worked as a department-store clerk, the Simpsons' total income was low. Their boys were already entering their college years, so finances were extremely tight. Aubrey's deep insecurity manifested itself in an excessive dominance over all the family members. None of the boys felt close to their father.

Pam was upset with Aubrey about something most of the time. Her main complaint was the low family income. Aubrey couldn't seem to make much money on the farm since it was rather small and prices for crops and cattle had been low in recent years. His mechanic skills were not being put to maximum use since he couldn't seem to hold a job for long with any of the local garages. Most days Aubrey stayed home fixing the fences and reading his "preacher books." He was afraid to go after additional work in town since he had been laid off so many times.

In counseling, Pam would often say, "I've never known anyone so insecure." When suggestions were made concerning possible job opportunities to increase the family income, Aubrey would usually begin his response by saying, "Well, I'm afraid that . . ." and come up with several reasons (excuses) why none of them would work out for him. His ultimate goal in life was, as he put it, to become an institutional chaplain in a prison or hospital setting. Since he was qualified academically, he was advised to prepare a detailed biographical resumé to be used in making applications for chaplaincy openings. After months of counseling, he never completed the resumé. He was always "working on it." Aubrey was paying a heavy price for his self-image of insecurity: an unhappy and unfulfilling marriage, a constant shortage of money, a lack of respect from his sons, and a dying church with fewer and fewer people attending while he was pastor there. The "insecure" vision is indeed painful.

The "repulsive" label also carries a painful self-fulfilling prophecy. Earlene Cannon was reared by a moralistic and puritanical

mother. Her father was extremely passive, quiet, and unrespon-
sive in the home. He was, as Earlene said, a non-person who was
not allowed by his wife to have much say in family matters. His
main duty was to bring home the paycheck and fix things around
the house. Mother was convinced that God's love had to be earned
by good behavior. For her, the "unpardonable sin" was sex. She
felt that being female was a sort of built-in natural handicap, with
the menstrual cycle as a constant reminder of the Fall and original sin! One's body was something to be tolerated but covered at
all times. Earlene's sensuous female body made for double
trouble. It was no surprise that she came to view herself as "repulsive." Although highly moral by church and community standards, Earlene felt inwardly dirty because of her female traits and
endowments. Naturally, all boys were morally suspect, especially
in their sexual interests. Mother had been an effective teacher.

Earlene's relational problems surfaced after marriage. The
wedding ceremony and marriage license failed to remove her negative feelings toward her body and sex. Her husband, Steven, had
no idea that he had married a girl who had been conditioned to
see herself as "repulsive" and "dirty." It would have been a mira-
cle if they had not had sexual problems in their marriage. For
Earlene, sex was repulsive because her body was repulsive; this
dimension of life was ugly and dirty and could not be enjoyed.
Physical pleasure was "sinful," even in marriage. Sex was only
for having children. The negative views about sex of such early
church fathers as Tertullian and Augustine were still very much
alive in Earlene's upbringing, even though her mother had never
read the teachings of those ascetic "saints." Now a harvest of conflict and pain was reaped in Earlene and Steven's marriage. The
"repulsive" inner vision inevitably causes some degree of relational suffering.

Similar stories could be told regarding persons who wear the
personality label of "weak." In the last chapter, I mentioned the
case of a young woman who had learned in childhood that when
she was sick she received unusual attention and nurturing from
her parents. But later, as a mother and wife, this weak and sickly
role backfired in her marriage and home. Her extreme dependence left her no strength to give to others at home whose own
needs were being neglected by her. Only when her husband threatened to leave her and take the children with him was she willing to
seek help and to make some radical personality changes. In time,

self-chosen and unnecessary weakness and dependence become painful realities that will crumble most of one's interpersonal relationships.

The "angry" label on one's self-image will also produce interpersonal conflicts. James Roberts was a young and fired-up evangelistic pastor. Having recently been called to his first church, James quickly got the reputation of being an aggressive, exciting, and dynamic preacher. Large numbers of people came to his church just to experience his pulpit explosions each Sunday. But, in time, James's loud and angry preaching began to wear thin. Love and genuine compassion were obviously missing in this man's ministry. His charismatic outbursts in the pulpit made for sensational entertainment and interesting community chitchat during the week, but such antics were not meeting the needs of his people, and before long they realized this. They had a preacher (not a pastor in any sense of the word) who carried around with him a bag full of "mads" that he would dump on folks either in or out of the pulpit. His "John the Baptist" image of prophetic fire soon burned out as the people gradually realized that they would rather "see Jesus."

In a few months James's anger destroyed his relationships with his staff members (whom he ran off), the deacons (whom he sought to disband), and a growing number of other church members. Forced termination by the deacons brought down the curtain to his short ministry of authoritarian church rule. God-loving lay people are simply not going to put up with that much anger in a pastor for long. The entire scene, needless to say, was a very painful one for James, his family, and the entire church, whose reputation in the community was seriously damaged.

In like manner, the "judgmental" label invariably pays off in similar currency. Judgmental criticism as a lifestyle will have a boomerang effect. Paul wrote something about this law of behavior (see Rom. 2:1–3). Jason Miles, an appellate-court judge, was one of those picky perfectionistic persons who could never find anything good in anyone or anything around him. He criticized his wife, Rose, so mercilessly that she finally left him after eleven years of a marriage in which she honestly tried to meet his standards. But it finally dawned on her that Jason's love for her was clearly conditional. Her housekeeping, meal preparation, care of the children, performance in bed, the way she dressed and behaved in public, were never good enough for Jason. He could always read off his list of her faults from memory. He finally tore apart what love she ever had for him.

Now in her second year of a new marriage, Rose says her freedom from Jason's criticisms and her relationship with a husband who accepts her unconditionally have brought her a happiness she had never known before. Moreover, Rose's children by Jason have not been sick a single day since the divorce. The absence of stress from Jason's criticisms has seemingly cleared up various psychosomatic problems the children formerly had. In the meantime, Jason is living in the misery of his self-imposed loneliness. Of course, he continues to blame everyone but himself for his painful existence.

Similar case studies could be cited for those who bear the labels of "irresponsible," "boss," "V.I.P.," and "pious." Persons who are relationally "irresponsible," or who feel compelled to dominate ("boss") those around them, or who demand all the attention possible ("V.I.P.") from family and friends, or whose behavior is marked by a false humility or super-religious demeanor ("pious") will most likely end up in some kind of serious ongoing conflict in their interpersonal relationships. They will inevitably suffer the pain of isolation. For who wants to live and work with such people?

To Sum It Up

The big question, and the point of this chapter, is to ask those of you who have found yourself bearing one or more of these negative personality labels, "Are you tired of the pain—tired enough to want to do something constructive about it?" If you are "on the bottom" and hurt enough, you may be at the point of desperately wanting to change.

But let me warn you: change isn't easy and the human personality, especially an adult's, is strongly resistant to change. For most people, a radical change of one's personality is a frightening thought that may be stubbornly resisted. It has been my observation that only those who hurt enough and are tired of the pain will even entertain the idea of change.

What I am suggesting is the changing of your self-image. Is such a transformation possible? Read on.

_____ 6 ___

Can You Change
Your Self-Image?

At this point you may be seriously wondering whether change, that is, *radical* change, is possible. You may concede that some improvements may be attainable. But is deep, significant, and thorough-going change in one's self-image possible?

Most of us would agree that children are certainly susceptible to change, since they are relatively pliable, open, and willing to entertain new directions for their lives. But adults? "You can't teach an old dog new tricks" is a cliché. But we are not dogs and we're not talking about tricks. From a biblical perspective and especially as an evangelical Christian, it seems loud and clear to me that adults can change and change radically, deep within the personality, beginning at the core of the self-image.

Yes, You Can Change!

Not only does the Bible presume the possibility of change in the hearts and lives of human beings, but I have seen countless instances of people who have emerged from a vital confrontation with God and his revelation in Jesus Christ with a new vision of self and a new direction for life, manifested in changed behavior patterned after the character and likeness of Jesus Christ.

The Good News concerning Jesus Christ says, among other things, "Yes, you can change. You can be a new person. You can have and live a new life." In Christ, God offers us a new self and invites our cooperation in bringing it to reality. This means both that we can change and that we can *be* changed. God initiates and we cooperate. God vitalizes and we cultivate. Both are true. Paul described this dual process this way: "Therefore, my dear friends, as you have always obeyed . . . continue to work out your salvation with fear and trembling, for it is God who works in you to will and to act according to his good purpose" (Phil. 2:12–13). That is, change is a partnership wherein the divine and the human work together.

The new self-image that is possible for each of us from the Christian perspective is the vision we are given in a new self that replaces the old self. The old self could be dated B.C. ("before Christ") while the new self dates from A.D. (*anno Domini*, "in the year of the Lord"), or after Christ came. The coming of Christ into one's life makes the difference. Christ not only brings the forgiveness of the sins of one's past but a new vision of the self that he has begun to re-create to transform the present and the future.

Moreover, the new self in Christ is both a status and a process, a gift and a task. Paul often balances these two facets of salvation. In Ephesians he describes the new status as our having been "raised" and "seated" with Christ (2:6), while the process is described as a "workmanship" doing "good works" (2:10). Similarly, in Romans Paul portrays the new status as "a righteousness from God" (righteousness = right standing), "a righteousness that is by faith" (1:17; cf. 3:21–22), while the process is envisioned as living "a new life" (6:4), as offering ourselves to God as "instruments of righteousness" (6:13) and as "living sacrifices (12:1), and being "transformed by the renewing of your mind" (12:2). Likewise, Paul contrasts the *gift* ("So then, just as you received Christ Jesus as Lord" [Col. 2:6]) with the *task* (". . . continue to live in him, rooted and built up in him, strengthened in the faith as you were taught" [Col. 2:6–7]). This pattern is seen all through Paul's letters as he explains the Christian life.

Moreover, the gospel of Christ offers a new script to go along with the new self. In a drama every actor plays a role, and each role follows a script. The script reflects the contents of the role, including not only the words to be spoken but also the beliefs, values, emotions, goals, and purpose of the role being played out. As the old self (role) is cast aside, the Christian puts on the new self (role), which involves a new script for the believer to follow. Change takes place as the new script is learned. Again, a new status/gift is offered (the new role) along with the process/task (the new script to be learned and acted out on the stage of life). The dynamic of the change is not merely conceptual but also experiential, as God is moving and empowering the believer throughout the entire endeavor. Yes, by the plan and power of God, you can change your self-image. The following section is an attempt to show how it can happen. A variety of possibilities for change exists. Some approaches are helpful but limited. Some tend to be man-centered, others God-centered. Some are short-term, others permanent. You will notice the differences, yet hopefully gain something from each approach.

Human Strategies for Change

There are several strategies for changing one's self-image and an element of truth is in each, though we need the total picture before us to recognize something of a pattern for change. Even "being saved" does not reveal the whole story. Just because you become a Christian does not guarantee that your self-image will automatically be changed overnight. There are many Christians who continue to live with a poor or negative self-image. Why is this so? The following scripts are effective so far as they go, but each strategy lacks an essential ingredient, the element needed for total and long-lasting change.

Avoiding the Problem

For one thing, many true believers simply avoid the problem of their self-image. To be "saved and headed for heaven" is sufficient for these naive and immature folk. For them, no change of any deep significance seems really needed. Being "born again" is enough—just don't push them about what being "born again" implies regarding the totality of one's life. They now bear the name

Christian, attend church, pray, read the Bible, engage in various church responsibilities, and live a good moral life in the community. The trappings of faith are observable. What else is needed? This strategy for change is only superficial and lacks any depth regarding one's basic personality or vision of self. But it probably describes a majority of contemporary church members.

Reformation or Self-Improvement

Another strategy for change might simply be called reformation. This is a man-centered focus on self-improvement and is a very popular approach today. If you have visited any of the major secular bookstores in recent years, you are no doubt familiar with those large sections of the store marked "psychology," "personal growth," or "self-help." The so-called self-help books have been selling quite well, and there are a lot of different titles covering a multitude of personal problems, the solutions to which people are desperately seeking. Although the majority of such books are "secular," a growing percentage in recent years has a distinctively "religious" orientation.

There is certainly some value in a person with serious problems trying to do something about him or herself. There is some truth in the idea that although you cannot change other people in your life, you can do something about changing yourself—assuming you are aware of the nature of your problems. But there are dangers and limitations to mere reformation. Improving one's self-image is not as easy and simple as some authors seem to suggest. It seems doubtful to me that humans can radically alter their personalities by themselves.

Jesus seemed to warn us against even trying this approach:

> "When an evil spirit comes out of a man, it goes through arid places seeking rest and does not find it. Then it says, 'I will return to the house I left.' When it arrives, it finds the house unoccupied, swept clean and put in order. Then it goes and takes with it seven other spirits more wicked than itself, and they go in and live there. And the final condition of that man is worse than the first" (Matt. 12:43–45).

Could it be that Jesus was suggesting that humans, by themselves, have nothing with which to replace the old self (with its sinful nature and poor self-image), at least nothing that is permanent, healthy, and spiritually strong? Notice Jesus' description of the house as "unoccupied." Without God, humans cannot find any ultimate solutions to their deepest inner emotional, relational, and spiritual problems. At the core of the human's personality and self-image problems is a vacuum that only God can fill.

Self-improvement may clean up and temporarily re-arrange a person's thoughts, feelings, values, intentions, motives, goals, and behavior. But if God's plan for a permanent and ultimate replacement by way of spiritual transformation is bypassed or ignored, eventually problems return that are worse than the original. *"And the final condition of that man is worse that the first."*

I have counseled many alcoholics, drug addicts, chronically depressed folk, and societal or family dropouts who testified that they had tried for years to solve their inner problems on their own. It was as if they had chosen for their life's theme song "I Did It My Way," but they were worse off than when they had first sought to change. No efforts on their own had really worked, and now they were at the bottom, on their backs, so to speak, looking up and crying for help.

Education, Information, or Insight

Another human strategy for change involves learning as much about yourself and your problems as is possible. This approach assumes that change will automatically take place by means of education, information, and insight. Now there is some truth here also. It is a truism that ignorance never precipitates permanent and constructive change. Ignorance usually blocks or prevents any significant change in one's life. The well-known inscription on the temple of Apollo at Delphi "Know thyself" is basically sound. Jesus and the biblical writers presumed that a true knowledge of oneself in light of God's revelation of himself was an important and good thing to have. The New Testament has much to say about knowing, thinking, and believing correctly regarding one's true condition before God. Clearing away the underbrush of ignorance about yourself is always an important preliminary step toward change.

But you can read all the books on psychology, self-image, and human behavior; you can take all the personality inventory tests there are to take; you can seek all the interpretation by experts of your behavior patterns that you can afford; you can gain all the insight possible into your inner motives and drives—and you will still not make any significant or permanent change in your self-image. Facts do not necessarily move one to change. Thomas Aquinas did not speak solid experiential truth when he wrote, "To know the good is to do the good." Most humans already know better than they are doing! Information does not often touch one's will or emotions, wherein lies the dynamic for change.

But do not misunderstand me. As an educator, I believe in the search for truth, the gaining of insight, and the accumulation of and accessibility to correct information about oneself. But more than facts and interpretations is required to bring about a radical change in your self-image. Information is like natural gas in a heating system. It is absolutely necessary to produce a change in the temperature, yet it must be ignited and its heat properly directed before any change takes place.

Counseling

A very important and helpful strategy for change is the use of counseling at the hands of a competent and skillful therapist. Psychotherapy has come a long way in recent years in helping persons bring about needed change in their lives. Of course, as in any profession, there are quacks who do not know what they are doing and only want your money. Counseling in several states is unregulated, so would-be "counselors" can simply "hang up their shingle," identifying themselves as "counselor," "psychologist," "psychotherapist," or something similar, and with a sometimes-bogus doctoral degree go into the business of counseling. Regulation by law is coming in a growing number of states, but slowly. In the meantime a lot of desperate people may be receiving less than adequate treatment from insufficiently trained counselors.

Competent counseling can be a lifesaver. Counseling can be extremely beneficial if it helps a person identify the nature of the problems being faced, understand something of the causes of the inner turmoil and outer conflict being experienced, and work through the emotions that are stirring within. With that as a foundation, a counselee is better able to recognize and weigh the alternatives for action, get a handle on making the best available decision for change, and receive the emotional support needed to follow through.

Yet even good counseling is no guarantee that one's self-image can be changed thereby. Whether short-term or long-term, counseling may only assist a person in dealing constructively with solving some immediate emotional and relational problems. This may only be temporary at best.

However, some relief is better than none. To change one's self-image by way of intensive counseling calls for a most unusual therapist who is competently trained to use a unique set of conceptual tools that reflects an understanding of how humans are made and function, and thus will address the emotional, mental, relational, and spiritual nature of a self-image problem. The following strategy is offered with the conviction that it meets such criteria. The remainder of this chapter will set forth the psychological and theological rationale for this strategy, while the following chapter will present the dynamics involved in how such change can take place.

Changing the Labels

The particulars of labeling theory were presented in an earlier chapter. Simply stated, it begins with Alfred Adler's theorizing that each person wears certain labels of identity. These personality labels are based upon self-perception. In addition, the labels function as one's behavioral goals. Since all behavior is goal-oriented, the labels of self-perception become the directional determiners of one's feelings and actions. Therefore, if you want to change your behavior, you must change your goals, which involves changing the labels you wear concerning yourself. The same idea applies to changing your overall self-image. Your inner vision of self is changed by changing the labels of your identity.

To change your labels, however, you need to identify the labels you currently wear. Adler suggested that one way to do this is to examine and interpret your early memories, those consciously recalled that happened before the age of six, and the earlier the better. The use of early memories is a sort of "projection" technique. That is, you project into and out of the early memories the nature and character of your self-image in symbolic fashion. Of the thousands of things that happened to you as a small child, why is it that you recall only a very few experiences, and why these particular ones and not others? Adler theorized that your mind reaches

98

into the subconscious and selects certain events for recall because these recollections reflect the way you see yourself, the world around you, and even "life" in a broader sense. Your early memories also need to be studied in light of your birth order (oldest, middle, youngest, or only child), since birth order partially provides the raw materials for how you make a place for yourself in the family. This is directly connected with the development of one's self-image.

I received my training in Adlerian psychology during my graduate studies at Texas Tech University in the late 1960s under the direction of the late Dr. Ted Andreychuck, then professor and chairman of the department of psychology. Since that time, I have studied the early memories of well over three hundred persons in my counseling ministry. This approach has been an amazingly helpful tool in understanding the self-image and in precipitating change in human behavior. (Unfortunately, there is very little written on this subject for lay readers; most research published on early memories is found only in certain professional psychology journals not easily accessible to most people. See Harold H. Mozak, "Early Recollections as a Projective Technique," *Journal of Projective Techniques*, Vol. 22, No. 3 [1958], 302–311. See References for additional articles.) At this point, an illustration would be helpful.

Betty Dickson, discussed in chapter five, sixteen years of age, had been giving her parents considerable trouble in recent years: fits of temper, using extreme profanity and throwing furniture around when angry, doing poorly in certain classes at school even though she was exceptionally bright, daring her parents to punish her, staying out much later than agreed upon, talking back disrespectfully to her parents and teachers. Betty had seen a psychiatrist off and on for over two years who finally recommended hospitalization if she did not control her behavior. Betty was adopted when she was sixteen months old and was the only child until she was nine, when her adoptive parents adopted her brother, Jim, then eleven. Her natural mother, an emotionally unstable woman, gave Betty up at three months. Betty then lived in a series of foster homes until adopted thirteen months later. Therefore, Betty did not have the normal, healthy experience of "bonding" with a permanent mother during her first year. When her parents brought her to me for counseling, I asked her to write out several early memories with as much detail as she could remember. Here is what Betty recalled:

At sixteen months: "I had a bad sore throat the day I came to live with my folks. Some lady brought me in. She handed me to my new Dad. I was screaming and crying because my throat hurt so bad." (It is rare for someone to recall an event this early in life.)

At seventeen months: "I remember getting my picture taken for the first time. I had on a blue dress that day. Some man sat me up on a carpeted box and had a box of toys in his arms. He'd hand me a toy out of it and take my picture with it."

At two years: "My dog, Daisy, had puppies. I ran outside as soon as Dad told me. I went over to the doghouse and looked inside. Dad followed me out. I pointed at them and said, 'They have "bleed" all over them.' I hadn't learned to say blood correctly, I guess, but the puppies were newborn and they were kind of messy."

At three years: "I was in the hayloft of my uncle's barn with my uncle. I saw two mice sniffing around by the wall. I snuck up on them and grabbed one by the tail. I held it up and showed my uncle. He told me to put it down. Then the mouse curled up and bit my finger."

At three years: "I was in the car with my Dad and we were on the way to a distant city. I couldn't get a knot out of the ties on one of my doll dresses. So I put the knot between my teeth and yanked real hard. One of my teeth flew out. Dad pulled over at some gas station to get some napkins. While he was out of the car I looked into the mirror and opened my mouth. I saw all this blood pour out of my mouth. That's when I started crying."

At four years: "My parents and I were at this lady's house. She owned a doberman dog. It was huge. It opened its mouth, and I stuck my head inside. I was never scared of animals. I guess I must have hurt it somehow because it bit me across the forehead."

At five years: "I remember my first cuss word. A boy taught it to me. After school I came running into the house. I stopped on the wood floor opposite my Dad, who was resting in the green recliner. I stamped my foot and yelled, 'Oh, shad!' I was lucky I'd learned it wrong. Dad laughed."

Here is a very bright young woman who remembers vivid details. Her memories reflect those of an only child who seeks to be the center of attention, striving for approval. However, a "victim" syndrome appears here. Notice the blood, pain, getting bitten. She sees herself "getting the raw end of the deal," and as one who is often getting hurt. Themes of insecurity and rejection tend to prevail in her memories. This causes her to take a defensive position which is now expressed in angry behavior. Betty has a great fear of "being dumped again," as she was before being adopted.

Betty desperately wants to be loved and accepted, but she sees herself as basically "insecure" and "rejected." These have become her behavioral goals, and she is trying to reach them and prove they are true. She feels lonely and on the losing end of life. Remember that quite early she lost her natural mother and then a series of foster parents. Then, at age nine, she lost her favored only-child position when Jim came to live with them. Jim, being older, was a "threat," a "bossy kid," who "made me mad." Betty felt dethroned, a form of rejection. She has observed that "nothing ever stays the same," an expression of insecurity.

Such an interpretation helped Betty to recognize some of the dynamics behind her antisocial and rebellious behavior. In time she began to establish a new self-image of "secure" and "loved" ("accepted"), which in turn motivated her toward new and constructive behavior patterns. Her anger diminished greatly, her grades at school went to straight A's, and she became much more cooperative and congenial to be around both at home and at school. Betty moved from a negative to a positive self-image. Without going into detail here, it is important to say at this point that Betty was a Christian and had some understanding of the concepts of her Christian faith, which later became the conceptual basis for the changes she experienced. As she changed her self-image labels, Betty was able to experience behavioral changes. A positive self-image became her new life goal, and out of this flowed the higher self-esteem that cultivated new constructive directions for her actions.

I have intentionally avoided referring to the methods of biblical teaching and preaching in changing one's self-image. You do not have to be a Christian of many years to know that a lot of teaching and preaching in the church effects little if any change in people's lives. These methods have some of the same potential limitations as does counseling. Unless the approach focuses upon the biblical process of replacing the labels, there is little probability for lasting change. The changing power of the gospel of Christ is to be found in the nature of the message itself (Cor. 1:18), not in some special method. Change comes about from a new identity, being "in Christ" (2 Cor. 5:17).

From Self-Image to God-Image to Image of God

Does the Christian faith have anything to say about changing one's identity labels? Yes, most definitely so. There are three separate but overlapping steps involved.

Called to Look at "Self"

If you can change your self-image, where do you start? Well, you obviously start with your "self!" With an open Bible, you let the Word of God function as a mirror. The gospel of Jesus Christ calls you to take a good look at yourself. Look in the Scriptures and there you are!

Biblical stories, records of events, explanations, laws, commandments, poetic reflections, wisdom sayings, prophetic messages, Gospel accounts, apostolic letters, apocalyptic symbolisms, and historical interpretations tell us what God was doing for several hundreds of years with and through his special people: Israel and the early church, but especially in his Son, Jesus Christ. Yet one of the primary functions of the Bible is to show us ourselves. Therefore, when you read the Bible, look for yourself. Otherwise, the Bible may be read in a cold and overly rational matter and for information only.

Man's self-image got off to a good start. The record of the creation of the first man and woman reveals that we were all made in the image of God: "So God created man in his own image, in the image of God he created him; male and female he created them" (Gen. 1:27).

But Genesis 3 records how man sinned and fell from his lofty status with God. And much of the remainder of the Bible tells the sordid story of man's sinful journey through life. So when you look for yourself in the Bible, you are immediately confronted with both ecstasy and agony. There is the wonderful reality of our creation at the hands of God: "God saw all that he had made, and it was very good" (Gen. 1:31). But there is also the reality of our sinful rebellion and disobedience:

> ... the woman ... took some [of the forbidden fruit] and ate it. She also gave some to her husband ... and he ate it. Then the eyes of both of them were opened. ... Then the man and his wife ... hid from the LORD God among the trees of the garden (Gen. 3:6–8)

Though made in the image of God, man has had a dark side from that day forward. The original image was marred, defaced, distorted, twisted, but not destroyed. It was and is a candidate for re-creation.

This helps to explain why humans naturally struggle with a negative self-image. Such is the effect of sin. It distorts and perverts God's original plan for humans to see themselves as God intended: created in his image and likeness. Eventually each one of us must face the reality of our personal sin before God. The solution, of course, is found in the re-creation made possible through the Good News of Jesus Christ.

But when is a knowledge of the reality of sin possible? At what age? Are children responsible for their sins? Are children sinners? Or are they merely stumbling along in their immaturity? Christian parents are certainly concerned about such questions. Consequently, we must face not only the reality of sin but the reality of nurture. Should parents facilitate the growth and development of their children's self-image? Or are the effects of sin already too deep to make any difference prior to the possibility of conversion?

Since the Bible has very little to say about the spiritual condition of children before God, we might tend to think that sin stalks man's life from the very beginning. Yet the child in Israel and the early church was always perceived as being in a family covenant of faith, not necessarily "saved," but "safe" in God's grace until an age of responsibility and accountability was reached. (See Matt. 11:25 (cf. Luke 10:21); Matt. 18:3–5 (cf. Mark 18:36–37; Luke 9:48); Matt. 19:13–15 (cf. Mark 10:13–16; Luke 18:15–17); Matt. 21:16 (Ps. 8:2). See also William L. Hendricks, *A Theology for Children* [Nashville: Broadman Press, 1980] for a helpful treatment of the difficult topic.)

It is my conviction that children should be encouraged from the very beginning of life to cultivate a good self-image. There is a tremendous advantage in having a healthy, nurturing experience in childhood in the context of the family environment. "Train a child in the way he should go, and when he is old he will not turn from it" (Prov. 22:6). The reality of nurture is a mix, both good and bad. A child's upbringing will not completely protect him or her from the effects of sin, no matter how fine a Christian home is provided. Yet healthy nurturing in such matters as God's love and provision, mankind's creation in God's image, and the child's inestimable value—seen so clearly in the death and resurrection of Christ— are realities that prepare the young heart's soil for the seed of the word of salvation at the proper time.

This implies that there is certainly the need for salvation: the provision and re-creation of a new self. Yet this universal need does not preclude the importance of wholesome nurturing in a healthy family environment. It has been my observation that children who have been encouraged in a Christian home to develop high self-esteem will tend to become more mature and wholesome believers, with fewer emotional, relational, moral, and spiritual hangups about themselves in adulthood.

Called to Look at God

The Good News of Jesus Christ also calls us to take a good look at God. Changing your self-image will never take place as long as you look only at yourself, concentrating only on you. The proper vision of God is the beginning point of change toward a new self. God, our Creator, is the starting point for change.

It is from God's revelation of himself that we learn who we are. From Moses' vision of the glory and presence of the Lord (Exod. 33:7–23; 34:29–35), to Isaiah's vision of God in the temple (Isa. 6:1), to Job's fresh sight of God (Job 42:5), to Jesus' Beatitude for the pure in heart who will be able to "see God" (Matt. 5:8), to Paul's insight that the "God who said, 'Let light shine out of darkness,' made his light shine in our hearts to give us the light of the knowledge of the glory of God in the face of Christ" (2 Cor. 4:6), there has been the discovery that it is the vision of God that shows us what we were intended to be.

The clearest and fullest picture of God, of course, is seen in Jesus Christ. As Paul said: "He is the image of the invisible God, the firstborn over all creation" (Col. 1:15), referring to his first-born rights of priority over creation, his preeminence and sovereignty. Similarly, the writer of Hebrews declared, "The Son is the radiance of God's glory and the exact representation of his being, sustaining all things by his powerful word. . . ." (1:3).

As we move from self-image to God-image, we discover who we are in Jesus Christ. I was made in the image of God, and when God reveals himself to me in the person of his Son, I see what I was intended to be in the mirror of God's nature and character.

Called to be Re-created in Christ

Moreover, the Good News of Jesus Christ reminds us that we are to be re-created in the image of God's Son. The ultimate change in one's self-image, therefore, must be a spiritual one, not merely a psychological self-alteration. The long-term goal for every human being is to be re-fashioned in the new image of God, which is Jesus Christ.

The gospel of Christ reminds us that we were created in the image of God. Exactly what does "image of God" mean?

Traditional interpretation of this term has suggested that since God has reason, emotion, and volition, so God's image in man means that man can reason, feel, and choose. There is truth in such a view, but I believe that the biblical understanding of human sexuality (remember that both male and female were created in the image of God [Gen. 1:27]) can also tell us something about the meaning of "image of God."

First, there is the idea of relationships. That is, the possibility of interpersonal relationships is contained in the image of God.

Second, there is the idea of creativity, as God gives to man and woman the power to create a new human life. The image of God makes it possible for humans to be creative.

Third, there is the idea of responsibility or stewardship. Our sexuality calls upon us to be responsible for what we create.

Fourth, there is the idea of aliveness. Sexuality involves the possibility of new life coming into being, in which man is to rejoice as a blessing from God. This aliveness suggests energy, joy, pleasure, humor, and the ability to be fruitful. The image of God is dynamic, not static.

Fifth, there is the idea of completeness or wholeness. The best in human sexuality calls for complementariness and harmony, not competition or conflict. The two become one in purpose and meaning. The image of God calls for wholeness, not fragmentation.

Sixth, there is the idea of revelation. Human sexuality involves in its ideal expression the revealing of two selves to each other. The image of God makes possible self-disclosure to others.

Seventh, there are the mutual ideas of giving and receiving. Human sexuality involves both. Being made in God's image makes it possible for humans both to give and to receive. (For a helpful insight into the relational aspects of the image of God, see Anthony A. Hoekema, *Created in God's Image* [Grand Rapids: Wm. B. Eerdmans Pub. Co., 1986], pp. 66–111.)

As we know, however, sin marred the image of God. The effects of sin are clearly set forth in the Scriptures: spiritual blindness, deafness, crippledness, weakness, ignorance, and death—all manifested in a stark insensitivity to God. The call of the Good News is a call to be re-created in the image and likeness of Christ. The old image is replaced by a new one.

Although dealing with the nature and effects of the resurrection of Christ, Paul offered a general principle that applies to God's provision of a new self-image for his children: "And just as we have borne the likeness of the earthly man, so shall we bear the likeness of the man from heaven" (1 Cor. 15:49). God desires that this likeness of Christ be "formed" in his children (Gal. 4:19). If you want to change your self-image, I strongly suggest that you submit yourself to God for a self-image transplant: the new image of God in Christ.

To Sum It Up

Not only is a basic change in your self-image possible, but a variety of strategies for change exist. Beware of mere reformation, although there is an element of truth in the idea that you alone must determine to change your self. There is also value in learning as much about yourself as possible, clearing away the weeds of ignorance. It is no virtue to remain in the dark about yourself, but there are limits to what education can tell you on that subject. There is much to gain in competent counseling and psychotherapy at the hands of a spiritually sensitive and theologically informed Christian therapist who can help guide one toward authentic spiritual transformation. Yet some counseling can be so man-centered that it neglects the all-important factor of God's power in bringing about permanent and healthy change.

The gospel of Christ offers the believer a new set of identity labels to replace the old. These labels describe the believer's new status with God and become the new goals for a changed behavioral lifestyle. A new self is offered in Jesus Christ, a new image of God fashioned after the likeness of Christ. As we look at ourselves through Scripture, we see our dilemma, our need. But then, as we look at God in Christ, we see the possibilities for becoming a new person, re-created in that new image of God in Christ.

Some vital questions for the reader at this point are:

Do you really want to change?

What kind of change are you willing to undergo—that is, toward what?

How permanent do you want this change to be?

How deep do you want the change to go?

Do you want the change in your self-image to be man-centered or God-centered—that is, for what it will do for you or for the glory of God?

Do you want change that is short-term (until you can find something better or less costly or less risky) or long-term and eternal (total commitment whatever the cost)?

7

God's Plan for Change

　　God has a plan for changing your life. It is not merely reformation but transformation, not from below, "pulling yourself up by your own bootstraps," but from above, a divine intervention and invasion into one's life. This change is not a rearranging or improving of the old personality traits but the gradual and eventual replacement of the Old Self with the New Self.

　　For Paul, the ultimate in the Christian "mystery" was not only "Christ in you, the hope of glory" (Col. 1:27), but also Christ in you, the hope of a distinctively new life here and now. Simply put, God's plan for changing your life is "Christ in you."

A Personal Discovery

　　Let me use myself as an example of this process. (I hope that this does not seem egocentric and will not be understood as a "typical" experience.) For many years I had retained my childhood idea that becoming a Christian was merely making the right kind of religious "decision," after which God would give me the gift of salvation. The concept of "gift" suggested to me that salvation was some sort of earned reward that I could now carry around in my heart. This package of spiritual "goodies" would be all I would ever need—forgiveness of sins, eternal life, exemption from God's judgment and hell, entrance into heaven, ability to pray, the right to membership in the church, a good moral reputation, power to live the Christian life, and victory over temptation. My concept of salvation was clearly a static rather than a dynamic understanding, as I later learned. At nine years of age, this was apparently all I could understand about God's plan of redemption, but I held this simplistic view for several years.

It rarely occurred to me then that salvation involved a lifelong process of change in my attitudes and overall lifestyle. My graduate studies in theology opened my eyes to the realization that there is an ethical dimension to the experience of salvation to which I must respond on a deeper level. I had not seen much of that in the fundamentalistic environment of my early background, except with regard to moralistic prohibitions against alcohol and tobacco, dancing, promiscuous sex, certain movies, and other highly individualistic behaviorisms. There was almost no social ethic taught in the churches of my childhood, youth, and early adult years. For example, almost no one who influenced me during my formative years expressed concern for justice in race relations or in economic affairs, such as eliminating discrimination and the conditions that cause poverty.

In my middle-age years I carefully examined the teachings of those identified with the "Deeper Life" Movement (views of some charismatics and Ian Thomas, Jack Taylor, Peter Lord, and Watchman Nee) and quickly detected some obvious blank spots regarding what they believed about the Christian life. They also lacked any primary emphasis on social ethics and theological depth. (Actually, for them, theology was automatically suspect.) There was too much emphasis on the emotional dimension of human religious experience. Possessing the "right" biblical information, mainly knowing the appropriate biblical verses to support certain views on religious experience, was more important than relating those truths to interpersonal relationships in everyday life. The "Deeper Life" folks have much good to offer in counteracting the stale, dead, formal, lethargic, and relatively unhappy atmosphere in many churches. They know how to enjoy their faith. But a social conscience, an awareness of sin in social, political, economic, and religious structures, and an emphasis on the growth and development of Christian character tend to be missing in what they say and do. They also lack a strong commitment to the Christian missionary endeavor.

Next I examined the teachings of those who *do* stress social justice—those who make an effort to confront sin in social and economic structures, and who "struggle . . . against the rulers . . . the powers of this dark world and against the spiritual forces of evil . . ." (Eph. 6:12) in the political and economic arenas of society. Here I found any emphasis on self-image transformation, character development, and personal spiritual growth to be woefully missing, with some few exceptions. Such matters were considered too individualistic, pietistic, and psychological for serious consideration. Moreover, I discovered that those who tend to be more sociologically oriented can be quite arrogant in their views regarding how to change the world. Ironically, they are weak in both evangelism and missions.

When I examined the teachings of those who stress evangelism as the *summum bonum* of the church, to the neglect of other biblically mandated responsibilities, I found an overly simplistic "hot gospel" that pronounces that after a person is "born again" the rest of one's life will naturally take care of itself. For many folks on the fundamentalist end of the theological spectrum, social ethics are automatically suspect, sin is almost totally rooted in personal moralisms, and salvation is packaged as a sort of magical cure-all that comes with one's personal decision to receive Christ. It all supposedly happens suddenly at the end of "the sinner's prayer."

Though candidates for that all-important decision are quickly ushered into the baptistry, and certainly improve the statistical record of the pastor and/or evangelist, so often these same converts wander aimlessly months later. Guidance in discipleship, personal spiritual growth, and character development is lost somewhere in the shuffle of congregational activities, simply because such matters are not considered really important. This partly explains why, among the Southern Baptists' 14,000,000 registered members, over 4,000,000 cannot even be found.

One of the largest Baptist churches in the nation reports some 25,000 members but cannot expect more than 7,000 of them to attend in any one week. When a Romanian Baptist leader was visiting in the United States a short time ago and was told by the pastor what the average Sunday attendance was, he reportedly commented: "Sir, you have a very serious problem that would not be tolerated among the churches in my country." When asked, "What problem?" the Romanian responded, "The eighteen thousand who choose not to attend on Sundays! Most of them could not possibly understand the nature of Christian commitment and are obviously immature in their Christian faith." But this is a problem in most American evangelical churches. Evangelicals are good spiritual obstetricians but sloppy in their pediatrics!

I gradually realized that there had to be a better way to understand God's plan. Surely God's plan would be more life-changing and would somehow balance my conversion experience with my hunger for a "deeper life" with Christ through the Holy Spirit, my growing sensitivity to the needs of the less fortunate, the biblical call for social justice, and my growing love and understanding of the whole Bible. So I went to the Bible, equipped with forty-five years of experience with life, a growing personal relationship with Christ, and a concern for a balanced approach to divine transformation and growth. The following is what I discovered.

When God Takes Charge of Your Life

The Bible presents abundant evidence that when God takes charge of your life, he turns you around and takes you in a new direction. "Conversion" is one biblical concept that describes that experience. It is the act of repentance, faith, and turning to God noted in apostolic preaching (Acts 3:19; 2:37–39; 9:35; 11:21; 14:15; 15:19; 26:18). Jesus was talking about the same thing when he spoke of the necessity of being "born again" (John 3:3–8). Paul described it as a "washing of rebirth and renewal by the Holy Spirit" (Titus 3:5). Paul actually used many concepts, metaphors, and analogies to explain conversion to Jesus Christ: salvation, justification, redemption, sanctification, adoption, dying to sin and rising to new life, freedom from bondage, and called to be holy.

I learned that conversion is an act of God that creates in me a new way of thinking, acting, feeling, and valuing patterned after the nature and character of God as revealed in Jesus Christ. I discovered that the uniqueness of the Christian life is not to be found in a new way of doing certain "religious" things, like going to church, reading the Bible, praying, witnessing to the unconverted, and supporting church activities. Rather, I found that the Christian life offers a certain new way of doing *everything*. This new way is the way of Christ, and this taught me why it is so important for a believer to know the Gospel records regarding the way Christ thought, valued, felt, and acted. Of course, this includes the remainder of the New Testament as well: how the apostles interpreted the life of Christ for themselves and others.

Yet, as I discovered this approach, a probing question kept disturbing me. How does the process of change take place? How does God bring it about? It seemed to me that not knowing how God does it makes it more difficult for converts to cooperate and participate in the process. This was where my studies in the self-image and labeling theory offered a helpful interpretive key. Please don't misunderstand me at this point. In no way am I suggesting a "psychologizing" of the Christian faith. Rather, I am asking what the Bible and our experiences teach us about God's method for change.

Any careful student of the Bible knows that the Holy Spirit and the Word of God work hand-in-hand in the believer's life. The apostle Paul closely associated the Holy Spirit with the Word of God in the Christian's life (Eph. 6:17). Moreover, the work of the Holy Spirit in shaping the believer's new life in Christ is clearly connected with biblical truth as Paul explains this process in Romans (5:1–5; 8:1–17, 23, 26–27) and in Galatians (5:5–6, 16–18, 22–25).

How does the Holy Spirit use the Word in shaping the believer's new life in Christ? From my reading and study of the Scriptures and from my own personal experience, it is my judgment that beginning with conversion the Holy Spirit begins a process of relabeling the believer with the Word's own description of the identity of the child of God. The Spirit seeks, with the believer's cooperation, to strip off the old labels of the carnal "old man" (Col. 3:9, KJV). Here is how Paul puts it: "Do not lie to each other, since you have taken off your old self with its practices" (Col. 3:9). Then the Spirit empowers the believer to identify with new labels, to "put on the new self, which is being renewed in knowledge in the image of its Creator" (v. 10). Even the old cultural labels are rejected for the Christian, as the next verse pinpoints: "Here there is no Greek or Jew, circumcised or uncircumcised, barbarian, Scythian, slave or free, but Christ is all, and is in all" (v. 11).

Paul explains that Christ is the source of the new identity for the believer, and the process of renewal involves "the image of its Creator" (Col. 3:10). A string of new labels follows: holy, loved, compassionate, kind, humble, gentle, patient, forbearing, forgiving, loving, peaceful, and grateful (vv. 12–17). All this suggests to me that a new self-image is gained in the experience of salvation that is patterned after the image of God and restored in Christ, "the image of the invisible God, the firstborn over all creation" (Col. 1:15).

This same line of reasoning is followed in Ephesians. Paul says that the Ephesian believers did not come to know Christ in sensuality and impurity. Rather:

> Surely you heard of him and were taught in him in accordance with the truth that is in Jesus. You were taught, with regard to your former way of life, to put off your old self, which is being corrupted by its deceitful desires; to be made new in the attitude of your mind; and to put on the new self, created to be like God in true righteousness and holiness (Eph. 4:21–24).

The verses that follow contrast a string of negative labels with a selection of positive labels (see Eph. 4:25–5:21). These labels of the "new self" in Christ become the new behavioral goals toward which the believer strives in the power of the Holy Spirit (Eph. 6:10–18).

Daily Bible study is an absolute essential in the life of the growing Christian, since much meditative study reinforces the relabeling process on an ongoing basis. As God endows your life with a new identity, you are a "new creation" in Christ: "... the old has gone, the new has come! (2 Cor. 5:17). Your new self is identified by a new set of positive labels patterned after the image of God in Christ. Scripture provides an abundance of these affirming labels, which are motivational in that they provide positive behavioral goals toward which the believer strives. In the strength of the Spirit of God, the believer must prove that these new labels are true, and his or her behavior is now oriented around achieving the new goals. If you see yourself "in Christ," you have to prove that you are in fact "in Christ." As Paul put it: "Since we live by the

Spirit, let us keep step with the Spirit" (Gal. 5:25). What you see is what you do. Christian visionetics means seeing yourself "in Christ" and proving that your inner vision is true.

The "process" is just that: a continual dynamic, not a one-time decision. Consequently, Christian life involves ongoing spiritual growth. When God empowers you to change your life, he does so over a period of time, not in a brief moment where all is accomplished at once. (This will be further discussed in chapter eight.) Spiritual growth occurs as we reflect and respond to the process of divine inspired change.

In addition, as God changes your life, he sensitizes your conscience to the difference between right and wrong attitudes and behavior. Notice the lengthy treatment in Scripture of morality: vices to be shunned and virtues to be emulated. Moreover, God expands your perception and response regarding the needs of others. It begins to feel natural to love the rejected and unlovely, feed the hungry, pray for the sick to be healed, visit those in prison, care for the unfortunate, remove the barriers of prejudice, and generally strive for justice on behalf of the oppressed.

Therefore, when God changes your life, he not only prepares you for heaven, but he also prepares you for earth. (Read again in the Lord's Prayer: ". . . your will be done on earth as it is in heaven" [Matt. 6:10].) He does this by making you a "new person" with a changed vision of self and the world around you.

The Divine Strategy for Change

It is now time to outline the divine strategy for changing your life. This involves looking at the "plan of salvation" from another and broader perspective than the more traditional one, which emphasizes the initial decision for Christ to the neglect of the ongoing process of *following* him. After all, Jesus' imperative invitation was not merely "decide for me" but "follow me" (Matt. 4:19; 8:22; Mark 10:21; Luke 5:27; John 1:43; 21:19, 22). If churches, preachers, and lay evangelists would recapture this biblical emphasis, much of the shallow decision-only evangelism that is soon forgotten by many "converts" would be replaced by a call for a deep and abiding discipleship. Only that approach will build strong and stable churches with disciples who have a positive self-

image and are thereby more likely to attract others who are looking for a meaningful and permanent change in their lives.

Now, what are the observable steps in the divinely ordained
strategy for change?

1. *Awareness.* Becoming aware of the need and possibilities for
a change in one's life is the first step. It is hoped that the material
in chapter 4, "The Negative Self-Image"—especially in compari-
son with the content of chapter 3, "The Positive Self-Image"—will
help to raise the level of awareness of the need for a radical change
in your life.

I can just hear a traditional evangelist of the "old school" respond upon reading this: "Psychological hogwash! What folks
need to hear is that they are lost sinners and doomed for hell."
Well, though I agree theologically, that language does not cut it
with most of urbanized America. The biblical word *sin* so often
does not strike home to the majority of the people the churches
are trying to reach today. After all, "sin" is an English word that is
not in the functioning vocabulary of most unchurched people. It
merely translates the original term in the Greek New Testament,
hamartia, which literally means "missing the mark." It is my conviction that several of the labels of the negative self-image can
help unchurched people to realize the fact that they have missed
the mark with regard to the will of God for their lives. The driving
force behind a negative self-image—which includes such concepts as rejected, loser, irresponsible, repulsive, weak, hostile,
and judgmental—is that person's stubborn rebellion against God.
Anyone who faces life with a "do it *my* way" attitude is truly
"missing the mark," the biblical concept of sin.

Christians who sensitively talk with and listen to the unchurched people they know will quickly learn that these folks are
hurting badly deep inside. They feel the pain of guilt, insecurity,
depression, loneliness, frustration, rejection, a sense of loss, fear,
hostility, self-centeredness, and uncertainty. And, what's worse,
they don't know why they hurt or what to do about it.

Recognizing the need for a life change is meaningless unless
coupled with an awareness that a new life is possible by means of
the positive self-image revealed in a right relationship with God
through a personal commitment to Jesus Christ as Savior and
Lord of one's life. This is not "psychological hogwash" but "theological dynamite." If the Good News of Jesus Christ can change

your life at the very core of your personality, that is truly "the power of God" as described by Paul in Romans 1:16. My explanation of the positive self-image in chapter 3 is an attempt to describe exactly what happens deep inside you when God changes your life. When you become aware of such possibilities for change in your innermost personality, you will be motivated to move ahead.

2. *Identification.* The next step is to identify the new goals that are available "in Christ." This is where the Bible steps in to describe the positive labels offered "in Christ"—loved, valued, responsible, capable, free, secure, and many more. The destructive character of the old goals based on negative labels is seen when contrasted with the new goals that conversion provides. The new goals present a road map for the direction God wants you to take. In the person and character of Jesus Christ, the new goals are supremely incarnated, fleshed out, and personified for us to see and identify. Paul often used this basic principle of identification when he instructed believers to be or do such and such "as Christ" was or did (see Eph. 5:23, 25, 29).

3. *Motivation.* Human beings rarely change without some kind of significant motivation. Training in psychological counseling always includes a study of the human being's natural disposition to resist change. The human psyche has a belief system that includes the tenet that it is safer and more secure to remain as you are.

Then what is it that moves people off "dead center"? Why do they change their negative self-image to a positive and Christ-centered one? The answer is very simple: God is the Motivator, yet he uses several means to move a person toward change. The gospel, the Good News of Jesus Christ, is God's primary source of motivation. Jesus was speaking of this motivating force when he said, "But I, when I am lifted up from the earth [his death on the cross], will draw all men to myself" (John 12:32). The story of Jesus of Nazareth as interpreted in the New Testament by the apostles and early church is the means whereby God confronts human beings with the promise of a new life. This new life is a new way of thinking, valuing, feeling, and acting, which is patterned after the person and character of Jesus Christ. This is actually what the New Testament is all about.

The second means God uses to motivate persons toward change

is to use selected major life experiences, both past and present, as spiritual levers. It is part of the work of the Holy Spirit to "convict" one toward conversion (see John 16:7–11). The pain of one's past, the frustration of one's present, and the uncertainty of one's future are used by God to move a person toward change.

The great majority of people I have dealt with in personal evangelism and counseling who have accepted Jesus Christ as their Lord and Savior have done so largely out of a desperate need to be released from the pain, frustration, and uncertainty of one or more difficult experiences. "No pain, no gain." It is sad but true that most people, especially adults, have to hurt a lot before they will seek radical change in their lives. Without a doubt, this vividly illustrates sin's enslaving power. Sin is a bondage that resists change. Only God can empower you to break those chains of resistance and set in motion the divine transformation of self.

I am not talking about what we used to call "foxhole conversions," motivated only by fear and thus short-lived. I have seen some "deathbed converts" pull through their illness and never follow through on their decision for Christ afterwards. Such "conversions" are based on a shallow, decision-oriented faith. Is this not what Jesus was talking about in the parable of the sower? The seed that falls along the path and is eaten by the birds, the seed that falls on rocky places where the soil is shallow, and the seeds that falls among thorns and is choked to death imply a short-lived faith based upon a quick once-only decision without follow-through (see Matt. 13:3–10, 18–23). Motivation without cultivation leads to dissipation.

4. *Neo-labeling.* Since I have discussed labeling theory and the self-image in previous chapters, I will state here only briefly that God's strategy for changing a life involves the process of re-labeling at the core of one's personality. As we have seen, the self-image is made up of a cluster of identifying labels. Change involves a replacement of the old labels with new ones. The old labels are produced by a combination of one's sin nature and a fallen environment, what the Bible calls "the world" (1 John 2:15–17; 5:3–5). The new labels come from and through the gospel of Jesus Christ. Through faith in the grace of God as revealed in the Good News, believers become new persons and gain a new identity and character.

Together, the Spirit and the Word impact the core of the believer's personality, impressing therein a new self-image. The results include (1) a new status with God; (2) a new script for living the Christian life; and (3) a new power for living this new life. The Word and the Spirit provide the two necessary ingredients for the Christian life: pattern and power. The pattern is revealed in the life, teachings, and character of Jesus Christ, primarily found in the Gospels but elaborated, explained, and applied in the other apostolic writings. Both the model (the life of Jesus) and the motivation (the power of the Holy Spirit) are needed to bring about divine transformation in one's life. The pattern of Jesus' lifestyle becomes the believer's new life-goal. The power of the Spirit's presence provides the motivation that makes the transformation a possibility. The new labels, set forth in the scriptural revelation, flow out of the person of Jesus Christ. These are found all through the biblical text, and every description of a follower of Jesus Christ is a positive and affirming label of identity. The positive labels discussed previously were derived from biblical texts regarding the nature and character of the child of God.

First, when a person becomes a Christian, he or she is given a new status with God: "righteous" (Rom. 1:17). This new status is explained in many biblical passages by such terms as born again, forgiven, reconciled, renewed, made alive, cleansed, sanctified, justified, washed, regenerated, set free, adopted, saved, sealed, rescued, and redeemed.

As part of that new status, the believer is given a new script for living the Christian life. This set of "instructions"—the teaching of Jesus and the apostles (Matt. 28:20; Acts 2:42; 1 Cor. 14:31)—is set forth throughout the New Testament to be read, studied, and internalized daily. The script guides us in not only what to *be* as persons but also in what to *do* in our behavior toward others.

Finally, the Christian is given a new power by which to live that new life "in Christ." This new dynamic is the power of the Holy Spirit, who resides in the heart of every true believer. No person can live the Christ-life in his or her own strength. The Christian life is Jesus Christ living in and through the yielded life of the believer.

5. *Personal yet social.* Becoming a Christian and living the Christian life are intensely personal experiences. Faith is a personal act of trust in and commitment to Jesus Christ. Yet God's plan for changing a person's life is also intensely social. The new

self becomes part of the fellowship of faith, a member of the body of Christ, his church. A Christian is a citizen of a kingdom, and the new citizenship entails considerable social and public responsibilities. The social dimension of faith is made possible because salvation in Jesus Christ includes the transformation of your social roles, not just the salvation of your soul.

When God changes a person, he alters the whole person, including that individual's variety of relational roles: male or female, husband or wife, father or mother, son or daughter, brother or sister, grandparent, relative of one sort or another, employer or employee (or whatever one's vocational role is), customer or clerk, citizen/voter/political person, neighbor, church member, club member, racial or cultural group member, and so on. Salvation is not something we act out in church but forget at home or in the community. If becoming a believer does not make you a *Christian* spouse, parent, and citizen, your profession is false.

Of course, it takes time for the process of redemption to penetrate all one's social roles. For example, Christian conversion did not remove my racial prejudice overnight, nor my struggle with sexual lust, nor my battle with economic greed, nor my indifference toward my political responsibilities. My conversion was only the beginning, not the end. (I will deal with this in chapter 8, "The Growth Factor.")

Overall then, the divine strategy for change includes the redemption of personal character (personality), the transformation of social roles (relationships), the conversion of behavior patterns (actions), the alteration of basic attitudes (sentiments), the mastery of human emotions (feelings), and the redirection of volitional choices (decision-making). All of this begins to happen slowly but surely when you become a new person in Christ, thereby gaining a new self-image.

A Theology for a Christian Self-Image

Behind the divine strategy for change is a theology for the creation of a Christian self-image. The following is an attempt to describe my own theological reflection of that reality.

1. *I have been created in the image of God.* This means that I can reason, feel, and choose. This gives me the capacity for relationships, the ability to be creative, the inner imperative to be respon-

sible, the dynamic of aliveness, the necessity for completeness and wholeness, the power of interpersonal revelation, and the mutual interplay of giving to and receiving from others. Being in the image of God means that I am more than an animal. I am a spiritual person with an eternal dimension and goal. I have the capacity to relate to God in a meaningful fellowship in a spiritual family kind of relationship.

2. *When I examine Jesus' evaluation of his followers, I observe something very special.* He gave them a positive identity and evaluation. He laid a special claim upon each one, enhanced, affirmed, uplifted, and valued each in the highest terms. He did not spend his time running them down, criticizing them, condemning them, categorizing them as bad, good-for nothing, or worthless. Rather, he highly valued his disciples and considered each one of inestimable worth. Jesus still does this today with his followers. I have every right to feel this same evaluation of myself as one of his contemporary disciples.

3. *Christ died for me, a sinner, because of his unlimited, unconditional love.* In spite of my sin, he values me so much to give himself ultimately, sacrificially, and completely. The cross of Christ is a constant reminder that I am worth dying for. Therefore, I have no right to devalue, detest, reject, despise, or hate what God loves so much that he would give his Son to die for. God's unconditional love for me enables me to love myself. Paul expressed it this way: "But God demonstrates his own love for us in this: While we were still sinners, Christ died for us" (Rom. 5:8; cf. 1 Peter 3:18; 1 John 3:16; 4:10).

4. *Christ rose from the dead for me.* This means that his new resurrection life is available to me and that there is unlimited power for living the new life in Christ. This is a resurrection-quality kind of life. John's Gospel calls this "eternal life" referring not merely to its enduring nature (life in hell is also eternal), but to the fact that it is a life *worth living* forever. Life in Christ is a quality of being that I can feel good about, relish in, enjoy, and celebrate. Speaking experientially regarding the present, Paul said, "I want to know Christ and the power of his resurrection . . ." (Phil. 3:10).

5. *Salvation means a "new creation" in Christ Jesus.* As a believer in Christ, I have a new self-image created in the image of Jesus Christ. Paul declared, "Therefore, if anyone is in Christ, he is a new creation; the old has gone, the new has come!" (2 Cor.

5:17). He also said, "Neither circumcision nor uncircumcision means anything; what counts is a new creation" (Gal. 6:15). That is, adherence to external religious rules or ceremonies is meaningless without the inner transformation of one's personality by the power of Christ.

6. *Christian life involves being renewed after the likeness (image) of Jesus Christ.* Paul explained that believers have been made new in the attitude of their minds and have clothed themselves with a "new self," which has been "created to be like God in true righteousness and holiness" (Eph. 4:24). Similarly, the apostle noted in Colossians that believers have been given a "new self, which is being renewed in knowledge in the image of its Creator" (Col. 3:10). This is a biblical expression of what we mean today by a new self-image. When the Christian sees him or herself, there is sound theological basis for seeing a new person who can be highly valued, esteemed, and affirmed. The old self is gone and a new self has come into being. This is not spiritual egotism or religious arrogance but biblical fact. As a new person in Jesus Christ I am to be respected, loved, and affirmed by myself. The new self is Christ being "formed" in every believer (Gal. 4:19).

7. *Christ-like character is an end product of God's redemptive process in my life.* This is one of the primary results of "Christ in you" (Col. 1:27). Character refers to the kind of person I am. It refers to moral excellence and firmness. Paul suggested that suffering for Christ can be one of the crucibles for character development when he wrote that "we know that suffering produces perseverance; perseverance, character; and character, hope" (Rom. 5:3–4).

The biblical word translated "character" refers to that which has been proved, tried, and approved after examination and trial. It has stood the test of time and experience. Therefore, character means those moral qualities or virtues—skills of the good life— that exemplify the kingdom of God.

The "virtue lists" of the New Testament illustrate these moral qualities. For example, Philippians 4:8 refers to whatever is true, honorable, right, pure, lovely, whatever is of good report, as well as things excellent and worthy of praise. Believers are "to think about such things," to dwell upon such virtues with the mind. Colossians 3:12–14 urges the people of God to clothe themselves with the virtues of compassion, kindness, humility, gentleness, patience, forbearance, forgiveness, and love. Similarly, 2 Peter 1:5–7 suggests adding these virtues to one's life: faith, goodness, knowledge, self-control, perseverance, godliness, brotherly kindness, and love.

The biblical "vice lists"—failures of the old life—state those opposite traits of character to be avoided and are sometimes contrasted with the virtues of the faithful life. A classic passage where this is done is Paul's "fruit of the Spirit" list: love, joy, peace, patience, kindness, goodness, faithfulness, gentleness, and self-control—compared with the "works of the flesh": sexual immorality, impurity, debauchery, idolatry, witchcraft, hatred, discord, jealousy, fits of rage, selfish ambition, dissensions, factions, envy, drunkenness, orgies, "and the like" (Gal. 5:19–23).

In the Gospels, the form of listing is different since it is set in the context of Jesus' style of teaching, but the classic example of a description of Christian character is the Sermon on the Mount, especially seen in the Beatitudes (Matt. 5:3–12) that introduce the entire sermon. Simply put, Christian character is a description of the nature of the new person in Christ.

To Sum It Up

The new self-image is a re-creation of the image of God in the Christian believer's heart. The old image, defaced by sin, is now restored, made new, and re-ordered to fulfill God's original plan for humans. The pattern for this transformation is the ongoing life of Jesus Christ, described in detail in Scripture, while the power is the personal presence of Jesus Christ, the Holy Spirit, in the believer's life. This divine presence brings the new self into being and seeks to cultivate it to its full potential. This is all made possible through the Good News brought to humanity by Jesus Christ. The gospel is God's plan for reconciliation and for changing your life. It is also God's great invitation to you to enter into this life-changing process. "Whosoever will, let him come!"

8

The Growth Factor

We have seen that developing a positive self-image begins with a valid experience with and a biblical understanding of the gospel of Jesus Christ. Since Christian faith is dynamic rather than static, a "process" perspective is an absolute essential. I call this "the growth factor."

The apostle Peter put it succinctly: "But grow in the grace and knowledge of our Lord and Savior Jesus Christ . . ." (2 Peter 3:18). What prompted Peter to state such an imperative was the lurking danger of false teachers who were distorting biblical truth in their attempts to lead believers astray. He noted that failure to grow could thereby result in spiritual disaster (v. 17). From such a warning, it seems to me that the apostle implies that spiritual growth is not merely a convenient option but an absolute essential for vital Christian discipleship.

Growth may be stimulated through involvement in a small group of growing Christians (as we will see in the next chapter), but growth must ultimately be initiated and experienced by the individual. In my own spiritual sojourn, I did not really begin to grow until I became aware of the *need* to grow and then *deter-*

mined to grow at whatever the cost. Awareness of need and personal determination are rooted in the law of growth. Without these two elements, spiritual growth will rarely, if ever, take place.

One's new self-image in Christ must be understood organically, not statically. As a believer, your new status with God through Christ is fixed and permanent. You have been "born again" into the family of God (see John 1:12). You are now a child of God and nothing can change that. Yet even the analogy of birth suggests that necessity for growth and thus the need for a new script and a new power. The script is provided by the labels of identity that define the goals toward which the believer seeks to grow. As we have seen, new labels transform your inner vision of self. What you see within becomes what you must do. The new power available in the presence of the Holy Spirit enables you to move toward the goals of your new identity. We are called to a higher level of being and doing, but responding to the call takes time, involves a process, and requires struggle.

Time Needed for Growth

There is no such thing as sudden "growth." The word itself suggests a continuing process. There may be a sudden turning in the direction of one's life, an instantaneous decision in the mind and heart to commit one's life to Jesus Christ—but Christian growth takes time.

The organic model of transforming one's self-image requires time. If you want something important to be permanent and stable, you had better invest a lot of time in achieving it, whatever "it" is. Someone once theorized that when God decided to grow a squash, he decided to take a few weeks, but when he chose to grow an oak tree, he planned to take several years. It all depends on what the ultimate objective is, when it comes to how much time it will take. Do you want a "squash" personality, or would you rather be an "oak"? It appears that our church membership rolls are full of "squash" converts who flourish initially, then fade, but only a few sturdy and abiding Christian "oaks."

The organic model of self-image transformation also suggests that the process of growth moves one from simple to complex, from elementary to advanced, from partial to complete, and from immature to mature. Several biblical passages suggest such a model for changing one's life. Paul told the Philippians that he was confident "that he [God] who began a good work in you will carry it on to completion until the day of Christ Jesus" (Phil. 1:6). Moreover, the apostle's prayer for them was that their love "may abound more and more in knowledge and depth of insight" (v. 9). Concerning himself, after expressing his longing for resurrection power in his life, Paul wrote in Philippians 3:12–14:

> Not that I have already obtained all this, or have already been made perfect, but I press on to take hold of that for which Christ Jesus took hold of me. Brothers, I do not consider myself yet to have taken hold of it. But one thing I do: Forgetting what is behind and straining toward what is ahead, I press on toward the goal to win the prize for which God has called me heavenward in Christ Jesus.

Paul told the Colossians that the ultimate goal of his ministry was to present all of his converts before God as mature in their relationship to Christ: "We proclaim him [Christ], admonishing and teaching everyone with all wisdom, so that we may present everyone perfect [Gk. *teleios*, "mature"] in Christ. To this end I labor struggling with all his energy, which so powerfully works in me" (Col. 1:28–29). Moreover, he admonished them, "So then, just as you received Christ Jesus as Lord, continue to live in him, rooted and built up in him strengthened in the faith as you were taught" (Col. 2:6–7).

Likewise, the writer to the Hebrews implored his readers: "Therefore let us leave the elementary teachings about Christ and go on to maturity, not laying again the foundation of repentence from acts that lead to death, and of faith in God, instruction about baptisms, the laying on of hands, the resurrection of the dead, and eternal judgment. And God permitting, we will do so" (Heb. 6:1–3).

There are numerous passages in the New Testament that strongly emphasize the importance of growth toward maturity. This progression involves not only one's relationship to God but also to oneself. It is my conviction that the growth of our new self-image in Christ is directly related to the growth of our relationship with God.

If time is needed for growth, there is an obvious need for patience. Growth invariably involves mistakes and failures. I once had a secretary who had made more than her share of goofs one day. She was simply having a "bad day," and nothing had seemed to go right for her. At the end of the day, she left a note taped to my door that read, "Dear Pastor, Please forgive me for all the mistakes I've made today. I don't know what was wrong with me. I promise to do better tomorrow. God isn't through with me yet!" That's true for all of us. We need to be patient with ourselves and others. God isn't through with us yet. He has a lot of unfinished business for each of us.

All Christians are in the growing business, and growth comes through our mistakes, faults, mix-ups, failures, and trial-and-error. When you were a child, how did you learn to walk? Did you wait until you were fully grown and an adult before you started trying? Of course not. You learned to walk as a child partly by stumbling and falling. Over a period of time you stumbled and fell less and less. Patience and determination went hand-in-hand and you gradually learned to walk. Shaping your new self-image is no different.

For growth to take place over time, there is also the need for pertinent experiences. Historian Arnold Toynbee's idea of "challenge and response" is suggestive here. For example, in the struggle to overcome racial or cultural prejudice, any existing prejudiced ideas or feelings need to be challenged, not so much with words but with experiences. If you live in a racially integrated neighborhood, attend a school of mixed ethnic backgrounds, belong to a church where races other than your own worship and serve, or work alongside those of other cultures at your job, this variety of experiences may challenge your prejudices. A Christian who is honestly seeking to live by the teachings of Jesus and the apostles will earnestly respond with changing attitudes of acceptance and respect for those who are "different" racially and culturally. This is neither easy nor instantaneous. But the response of change often requires the challenge of growth experiences.

Psychologist Erik Erikson taught that healthy growth and development require that the human person move through several stages of life ("The eight ages of man"). Each stage offers a particular developmental task that must be achieved or accomplished before one is ready to move on to the next stage. This developmental progression requires certain sequential growth experiences in order for the process of maturity to stay on schedule.

For example, the developmental task in adolescence is to achieve a sense of personal identity. Growth experiences that encourage a teenager to do this might include academic achievement in school, accomplishments in sports, wholesome experiences in dating, passing the exams for one's driver's license, religious conversion and church membership, wholesome experiences of pride in one's family name, and consistent affirmation from one's parents. Older adolescents attain further identity from graduation from high school, a scholarship award for college, gaining freedom-with-responsibility from parents over a period of time, and successful coping with interpersonal conflicts at school, church, home, or among peers. All these experiences become the bridge over which the person travels toward maturity.

Certain things need to happen to us before our growth can advance, and these experiences must come in God's good time. In a sense, God hides behind, beneath, or above these experiences to guide us toward maturity.

Can you think of any growth experiences that have happened to you in recent years? I can think of several in my recent adult years, including a nine-month Clinical Pastoral Education internship in a community mental-health hospital. There was also a very intense two-week course on personal and professional growth, directed by personnel of the pastoral ministry department of my denomination, in which one other pastor and myself participated in a radical evaluation of our personalities and ministries. Other challenges I faced include a five-year experience of pastoring a dynamic and rapidly growing congregation in a pioneer mission state; helping my daughter through some difficult times in her early adult years and seeing her achieve some very significant personal goals; being elected to the faculty of the theological seminary where I now teach; undergoing triple-bypass open-heart surgery and surviving; helping my wife walk through some serious vocational, physical, and emotional crises during a period of a few months; and teaching and working with national pastors and missionaries for several months in Argentina and Uruguay. The list could go on. Each experience moved me through one stage into another in the growth process, and time was the road upon which the experiences traveled.

Process and Not a Package

I have repeatedly said that the transformation of one's self-image involves a process. This emphasis is drastically needed in today's culture, where so many want "instant" benefits and blessings. Human growth and development never come in a neat package. You recall that one of the biblical terms describing God's changing of one's life is "salvation." Unfortunately, there is a brand of cheap and shallow evangelism today that offers salvation as part of a negotiated deal. The message is this: "If you repent of your sins and put your trust in Jesus as your Savior, then God will strike a spiritual bargain with you and save your soul from hell and for heaven." It sounds as if—in exchange for your repentance and faith—God gives you a sort of spiritual insurance policy.

Well, the truth of the matter is that salvation is not a deal but a relationship. God is not in the business of making crudely commercial spiritual bargains. He seeks fellowship with lost sinners. The late professor W. T. Conner of Southwestern Seminary, where I now teach, often defined salvation as fellowship with God. Through the gospel, God calls persons into a relationship of forgiveness and trust. This saving relationship, however, develops in a process, as all relationships do. Salvation is not a one-time-only decision of the past, seldom to be remembered except in church on such special occasions as testimony time during revivals. Salvation does have a beginning, but the relationship with God it signifies moves from acquaintance, to friendship, to an intimate fellowship that is close and meaningful. Since this fellowship always results in a positive transformation of who you are and what you are about, the growth factor is rooted in a relationship with God.

Growth also involves education, since it is a learning process. There is so much about ourselves we do not know. Looking back over my life, I must conclude that the amount of ignorance I carried with me about myself was staggering indeed. And I still have a lot of learning to do. But the point is, learning about yourself takes time; it, too, is a process. The truth about self, life, and God is not handed to you in a box that contains all the answers for you to carry around, nor even in the Bible, unless its content is studied and internalized into one's character.

When God changes your life, one method of change he uses is his teaching. Notice that a major role that Jesus played in the Gospel stories was that of teacher. Before his ascension back to heaven, Jesus commanded the apostles not only to make new disciples and baptize them, but to teach them to observe and obey all the things he had commanded (Matt. 28:19–20). The Sermon on the Mount ends with a strong injunction to hear and heed the words of Jesus (Matt. 7:24–27). In the conversion experience, the believer puts on a new self, the basis for a new self-image, but salvation requires that the new self be shaped and molded in a life-long learning process involving all the spiritual disciplines: Bible study, prayer, worship, fellowship with God and God's people, witnessing, sharing, caring, and an openness to God's revelation on a daily basis.

This learning must be assimilated or absorbed into the total fabric of one's personality. When God re-shapes your self-image, there is an integration process in which all the pieces of God's activity in your life are fitted together. It seems to me that Paul was dealing with something like this when he shared with the Corinthians how God had taken all the diverse and broken fragments of difficult experiences to teach him a very significant truth about the ultimate goal of the believer's life. Listen to the apostle's words in 2 Corinthians 7:4–11:

> But we have this treasure in jars of clay to show that this all-surpassing power is from God and not from us. We are hard pressed on every side, but not crushed; perplexed, but not in despair; persecuted, but not abandoned; struck down, but not destroyed. We always carry around in our body the death of Jesus, so that the life of Jesus may also be revealed in our body. For we who are alive are always being given over to death for Jesus' sake, so that his life may be revealed in our mortal body.

Think of it! The process of divine transformation at the core of one's personality involves assimilating and integrating all the problems and experiences of life toward one primary goal: the living and revealing of the very life of Jesus Christ in and through one's mortal body. We can conclude that God does not give us a new self-image merely so that we can feel good about ourselves and behave properly, but in order that Jesus Christ, "who is the image of God" (2 Cor. 4:4), might live through and be revealed in our lives. That is not spiritual egocentricity, but the normal Christian life.

The final result will be a great consummation: the salvation process is going somewhere very important. Paul described this so powerfully in Romans 8:18–21:

> I consider that our present sufferings are not worth comparing with the glory that will be revealed in us. The creation waits in eager expectation for the sons of God to be revealed. For the creation was subjected to frustration, not by its own choice, but by the will of the one who subjected it, in hope that the creation itself will be liberated from its bondage to decay and brought into the glorious freedom of the children of God.

The goal of the growth process is that the image of Christ be reproduced in the individual believer. You recall that God's salvation can be described in three time frames: past, present, and future. The future dimension stresses that our relationship with God is going somewhere. Paul spoke of pressing on toward this goal, the heavenly calling in Christ Jesus (Phil. 3:14). The growth factor involves movement toward the future, not stagnation in the present.

Struggle and Not a Downhill Slide

Growth and development of the new self-image in Christ involve struggle, hardship, and sometimes even pain. Growing "in the grace and knowledge of our Lord and Savior Jesus Christ" (2 Peter 3:18) is not some pleasant accident nor an easy downhill slide. Some folks want their growth in the Christian life to be like moving smoothly down a water slide in an amusement park. Biblically and experientially, that is not the case at all.

It seems to me that there is a natural built-in resistance factor in a Christian's old "carnal nature" (1 Cor. 3:1ff KJV; cf. Rom. 7:14ff), which Paul also calls the "old self" (Eph. 4:22). In more cases than not, as I counsel Christians who are seeking constructive change in their lives, I have learned that the resistance factor must be expected and overcome. Most people simply do not want to struggle in their desire to grow.

Yet struggle is the name of the game in the Christian "pilgrim's progress." The biblical writers often allude to this fact of life. The classic passage is Paul's discussion of the victorious Christian life, where he uses the metaphor of the "armor" of God: "For our struggle is not against flesh and blood, but against the rulers, against the authorities, against the powers of this dark world and against the spiritual forces of evil in the heavenly realms" (Eph. 6:12). Notice that the apostle calls the Christian life a "struggle," a word that can also mean a fight or battle. The writer of Hebrews also refers to his readers' efforts to live their new life in Christ as a "struggle against sin" (Heb. 12:4). Nowhere in the New Testament is there a suggestion that following Christ is a casual journey to heaven on flowery beds of ease. Rather, it is an uphill battle if there is any growth at all taking place.

A few years ago, at a statewide Texas Baptist summer evangelism rally for youth attended by several thousand teenagers, one of the speakers was that year's "Miss Teenage Texas." As she gave her Christian testimony, she was reported to have ended by saying, "Oh, young people, if you will only give your heart to Jesus and be saved, you will never have any more problems." Her intentions were good, but her experience and theology were immature and incorrect. Believers are not exempt from struggle and hardship. Jesus taught that both unbelievers and believers will experience the same difficulties and struggles of life, but the believers have a solid foundation and the resources to deal victoriously with them (Matt. 7:24–28).

There are several biblical models for growth. One is the normal slow process exemplified by the agricultural model of the growing seed. Although Paul was writing to and about the Corinthian church, the idea he presented applies to the growth principle for individuals, too: "What, after all, is Apollos? And what is Paul? Only servants, through whom you came to believe—as the Lord has assigned to each his task. I planted the seed, Apollos watered it, but God made it grow. So neither he who plants nor he who waters is anything, but only God, who makes things grow" (1 Cor. 3:5–7). Then Paul concludes the analogy with "you are God's field . . ." (v. 9).

Paul told the Colossians that his prayer for them was that they "may live a life worthy of the Lord and may please him in every way: bearing fruit in every good work, growing in the knowledge of God . . ." (Col. 1:10). Yet even the growth model in nature requires effort. Paul urges Timothy to "be strong in the grace that is in Christ Jesus," but he does so with this reminder. "The hardworking farmer should be the first to receive a share of the crops" (2 Tim. 2:1, 6).

A second biblical model of growth is the cross-carrying life of discipleship in following Jesus. Matthew records, "Then Jesus said to his disciples, 'If anyone would come after me, he must deny himself and take up his cross and follow me. For whoever wants to save his life will lose it, but whoever loses his life for me will find it' " (Matt. 16:24–25; cf. 10:37–39). Luke adds the word *daily* to the idea of cross-bearing (Luke 9:23). For Jesus, growth involves a daily denial of self (perhaps this is Paul's idea of the "old self") in the sense of rejecting selfishness and self-centeredness as one follows Jesus in the path of the new life. This path is clearly one of struggle.

A third model of spiritual growth in Scripture is that of warfare or conflict. The classic passage is Ephesians 6:10–18, where Paul presents the Christian life as a spiritual battle requiring the believer to be equipped with the "full armor of God" (v. 13). This armor includes "the belt of truth," "the breastplate of righteousness," with one's "feet fitted with the readiness that comes from the gospel of peace" (alluding to the protective and supportive footgear of the Roman soldier), "the shield of faith," "the helmet of salvation," and "the sword of the Spirit, which is the word of God" (vv. 14–17). It seems that prayer "in the Spirit" ties all the armor together and gives the necessary power to fend off the attacks of evil (v. 18). In a similar fashion, Paul tells Timothy to "endure hardship with us like a good soldier of Christ Jesus" (2 Tim. 2:3). Again we see that growth comes through struggle.

A fourth biblical model of growth is that of an athletic game or endeavor. Paul used terms straight out of the athletic world of his time to describe the Christian life. One term he used depicted being a combatant in the public games; another described contending, fighting, or striving earnestly. The apostle sometimes referred to his life in Christ as a race to be won (Gal. 2:2; 5:7; Phil. 2:16).

Two passages are of special importance here. First, Paul's

"pressing on," as described in Philippians 3:12–14, depicts a runner straining to reach the finish line:

> Not that I have already obtained all this, or have already been made perfect, but I press on to take hold of that for which Christ Jesus took hold of me. Brothers, I do not consider myself yet to have taken hold of it. But one thing I do: Forgetting what is behind and straining toward what is ahead, I press on toward the goal to win the prize for which God has called me heavenward in Christ Jesus.

The idea of "prize" came from the wreath of leaves that the winner of the Greek races received.

A similar idea is found in Paul's second passage on running, 1 Corinthians 9:24–26a:

> Do you not know that in a race all the runners run, but only one gets the prize? Run in such a way as to get the prize. Everyone who competes in the games goes into strict training. They do it to get a crown that will not last; but we do it to get a crown that will last forever. Therefore I do not run like a man running aimlessly . . . .

But then Paul brings in the metaphor of boxing: "I do not fight like a man beating the air. No, I beat my body and make it my slave so that after I have preached to others, I myself will not be disqualified for the prize" (vv. 26b–27). Growth for Paul involved the vigorous discipline of the victorious athlete.

A fifth model of growth is based on the construction of a building. Structures grow, brick by brick, board by board, beam by beam. Paul refers to Christians as "God's building" (1 Cor. 3:9b). Then he continues the building analogy with such terms as "foundation" and various kinds of materials used for the superstructure (vv. 10–15). Moreover, God's people are the temple of the Lord (vv. 16–17), which must be preserved. In addition, the followers of Christ are "God's household," which has a special foundation and superstructure that doubles as a "holy temple in the Lord" and "a dwelling in which God lives by his Spirit" (Eph. 2:19–22). The dwelling of God is also a "body" that must be "built up" so that "we will in all things grow up into him who is the Head, that is, Christ." The body "grows and builds itself up in love, as each part does its work" (Eph. 4:12–16). The concepts of building and body are blended, but the emphasis is upon the struggle of growth.

We can conclude from all of the above models that the growth factor of the new self in Christ involves struggle, work, engagement, striving, and determination. Growth does not come through the passive enjoyment of the pleasure brought by current benefits and blessings. Growth comes through the pain of exercise, which all athletes or soldiers understand during training. The "mountaintop experiences" involved in following and growing in Christ come only to those who *climb the mountain*!

The ultimate goal, of course, is the reproducing of the nature and character of Jesus Christ in the believer's heart and mind. Paul addressed the struggling Galatians as "My dear children, for whom I am again in the pains of childbirth until Christ is formed in you" (Gal. 4:19). The growth of the new self is a process of forming and shaping the person and character of Jesus Christ at the core of the believer's personality.

A similar way of stating this goal is found in Ephesians, where Paul teaches that pastors and teachers are to equip the people of God for the work of service or ministry, "so that the body of Christ may be built up until we all reach unity in the faith and in the knowledge of the Son of God and become mature, attaining to the whole measure of the fullness of Christ" (Eph. 4:12–13). This maturity—"the fullness of Christ"—is Christ being formed in believers. This idea is also found in Romans: "For those God foreknew he also predestined to be conformed to the likeness of his Son" (Rom. 8:29). Again, "Christ in you" is the "hope of glory," and this includes presenting "everyone perfect [mature] in Christ" (Col. 1:27–28).

To Sum It Up

Salvation is the making of a new person in the image of Christ. When God delivers us from our sins, Jesus Christ comes to live and reign in our hearts. The "old self" died with Christ on the cross and is now relegated to the past, stripped off and cast aside. The "new self" is put on like new clothes. This is an experience, a process, and a goal—all three—but the main emphasis in the New Testament is the growth factor. Believers in Christ are commanded to grow. It is an imperative, not an optional convenience that we can either take or leave.

In Christ, you are a new person. Now BECOME what you ARE!

9

We Need Each Other

God's plan for change was never intended to be a lonely endeavor. Since God made us social creatures, we need each other as we develop in humanness. Just as the biblical writers teach that sin has a social dimension, they also teach that salvation includes our involvement with our fellow humans. The change that God brings about in the human personality, which involves the acquiring of a new self-image in Christ, is more than a single, isolated event in one's past, a static one-time experience. Rather, as I have argued, it is a process, calling for ongoing growth. God's plan for such growth calls for a continuing social interaction with others of like faith—the body of Christ, the people of God—particularly in a local setting.

I don't think that my wife and I would have ever begun to grow as Christians to the degree that we have if it had not been for our relationship and involvement with a small group of close Christian friends. Participation in standard church organizational activities and our personal quest in private devotions were not enough. A careful study of the Bible slowly convinced us that we needed an intimate community of faith of like-minded believers in

Christ, a small support group wherein there was mutual accountability, encouragement, and fellowship that would stimulate the
growth of our new inner vision of self in relation to Jesus Christ.

A Support System

In discussing the growth and development of a new self-image
in Christ, the importance of close relationships cannot be over-
emphasized. The reflective capacity of the self continues to function throughout life. For a growing Christian this means that
other maturing believers are needed in a sustained and close context for one's "looking-glass self" to gain maximum benefits regarding a healthy Christ-centered perception. Earlier in this book
I discussed how we see ourselves reflected in the imagined evalua-
tions of our selves by the significant others who interact with us.
This suggests that it is very important that we surround ourselves
with persons who can enhance a positive inner vision of self in
Christ. Those people also need us for the same reason.

Consequently, I have discovered that a small group of interacting Christian friends that meets on a regular basis for prayer,
sharing, and fellowship can serve as an invaluable support group
in my quest for a maturing self-image in Christ. A Christian support group can provide a matrix of meaningful relationships that
stimulates the growth of my self-image. Our mutual experiences
in daily life offer a backdrop of helpful interpretation and evaluation of the self's responses to what is happening in and around
oneself. Such interpretation and evaluation can be quite a stimulus for healthy change.

The small support group was one primary method Jesus used
in the growth and development of his first disciples. A careful re-
reading of the Gospel records of the life of Jesus from this perspective revealed to me that Jesus planned his entire mission not
around a lonely quest for discovering and doing the will of his
heavenly Father but around twelve men with whom he would
share his life's purpose. His goal included the transformation of a
small group of willing followers into his character and likeness.

Jesus' ultimate plan involved the salvation of the entire human
race, yet such an awesome task needed to start somewhere. Jesus
chose to start with a small group. This small band of disciples became a mutual support group for each of them. There were prob-

lems, to be sure. They sometimes argued, disagreed, and worked
at cross-purposes with each other. One of them ended up a total
failure. But, all in all, they functioned as spiritual stimuli to each
other's growth and development. They matured in the context of
their relationships within the group's thoughts and actions.

If the small support group was so important to Jesus, why do
we so often avoid its use in the church today? Are we simply afraid
of closeness? The early church certainly saw its value. Beginning
with the Book of Acts in the New Testament and gleaning from the
pages of the letters of Paul, Peter, and the others, it seems obvious
to me that the first Christians followed Jesus' pattern for growing
and maturing people in faith and life.

For several decades, even possibly into the fourth century, the
Christian churches were essentially "house churches." In the earliest Christian writings there are such references as "the church
that meets in your home" (Philem. 2; cf. Rom. 16:5; 1 Cor. 16:19;
Col. 4:15). Apparently, many of the churches' activities took place
in private homes (Acts 2:46; 20:7), which strongly suggests that for
some time early Christianity was largely structured around small
groups, since most houses could not accommodate large crowds.
It was many years before congregations began to construct
"church buildings" as we think of them today.

I am convinced that a major problem or limitation of the modern church has been its movement away from home meetings and
small clusters of interacting believers. Rather, we have adopted
the lecture hall or auditorium model, with the underlying belief
that "bigger is better." The contemporary preacher is sometimes
tempted to lust after large audiences to massage or inflate his ego.
In the meantime, individuals get lost in the large crowd and rarely
experience the strength of the small support group for their own
growth and development.

Some churches occasionally recapture early Christianity's tra-
dition of recognizing the value and strength of the small group. A
study of general church history will reveal that whenever the
church was most vibrant its power was channeled through some
kind of small-group approach. One well-known example is John
Wesley's "holy clubs" at Oxford, which were the beginnings of the
Methodist Church as it moved out of a decadent and spiritually
lethargic Church of England in the latter 1700s. A study of Baptist
roots shows the use of small gatherings for prayer and Bible

study. The Sunday-school movement in general is the story of the use of small groups for Bible study even to this day. God seems to use this approach every time he revives the church.

On a more individual level, it is my contention that change in one's self-image calls for a new "reference group." You may recall from chapter 2 that a reference group is one that provides the standards and perspective regulating an individual's behavior within a given context, regardless of whether one is a member of the group or not. However, when you are an interacting member, the influence of the reference group is much greater upon your ways of thinking, valuing, acting, and feeling. So when you become a Christian and enter into the process of receiving and developing a new self-image, that process will be facilitated to a greater degree if you affiliate with a small support group of maturing believers on a sustained basis.

In my last pastorate in Los Alamos, New Mexico, from 1975 to 1980, I experienced and observed the molding power of reference groups, which we called "discipleship groups," in the lives of approximately 75 percent of the adult members. These groups served as the reference points for Christian values and provided a Christian perspective of life for those who participated. They also served as reference points of strength and encouragement for living a faithful Christian life. Incidentally, joining such new reference groups required cutting ties with certain former reference groups whose values and moral standards ran counter to those of the Christian faith.

Growth Through a Group

As the pastor of a church that was innovating with a small support group ministry, I felt the need to read everything I could lay my hands on that dealt with this subject. Several good books were in print and available at that time, both religious and secular. One book in particular was extremely helpful to us: *Growth Through Groups* by William Clemmons and Harvey Hester (Nashville: Broadman Press, 1974). It is now out-of-print but may be secured from some church, college, or seminary libraries. As far as finding similarly good books on small groups from a Christian perspective, you could consult your local Christian bookstore. What the Clemmons and Hester book did for us was to give us some clear guidelines for creating and sustaining small groups in the context of the church. The book also affirmed for us the conviction that personality growth can be greatly stimulated by the interaction of the small group.

Actually, several similar books provided us with a road map to growth through a support-group approach. Those of us who participated over a period of several years found the strength and dynamic for the growth of a positive Christ-centered self-image. The dynamics of affirmation and accountability in the group fueled the fires of positive personality change and the resulting growth.

What Groups Can and Cannot Do

It needs to be clearly stated here that small groups in the church are not a panacea. They have both strengths and weaknesses or limitations. We need each other, but the others in a small support group cannot solve all our personality problems.

A small group can do certain things for you. Assuming that some of the group's members have a measure of Christian maturity, the group can provide a Christian value system to serve as a "plumb line" to test one's own values. Where selfishness and greed unknowingly dominate one's thinking and acting, the group may serve as a check against such values. Where honesty and integrity have not consistently characterized one's past, the group may serve as a teacher and stimulus for such values. Where material values have generally overridden one's best judgments, the group may serve to point one in the direction of the spiritual use of material things or the subjugation of material things to spiritual goals in life.

A small group can serve as a theological teacher or clarifier of biblical truth. Where one's thinking about God and life has been fuzzy, confused, or in error, the group can serve as a source of instruction and correction. This is where new converts to the Christian faith can be helped tremendously about the meaning of Christian truth. The one-way lecture method of most Sunday-school classes generally lacks the dialogical dynamic of small-group interaction.

A small group can offer encouragement and support during times of difficulty and hardship. I will never forget the night when one of our group members in Los Alamos announced that he would be losing his job in a few weeks and was not sure where to turn for another position. John was obviously depressed. The members quickly expressed their encouragement and prayer support. It was an exciting day for the entire group when in a couple of weeks John called each member to say he had found another position at the laboratory and would not need to move elsewhere to find work. I have seen group members who were having serious problems with their teenage children reach out to the group for help. Ideas were shared by all, but primary encouragement and support would come from other parents of teens who had been through similar difficulties and found the courage to move on toward "the light at the end of the tunnel."

A small group can communicate a sense of value to members who happen to feel "worthless" due to either old personality hang-ups or recent circumstances. When a group is oriented around Christian love and appreciation, individual group members are more likely to come away from a session feeling, "I really am important; these people truly believe in me."

A small support group made up of active church members can give individual members a closer sense of identity with the congregational whole. Many churches in urban areas tend to be so large that it is difficult if not impossible to know very many other believers in the congregation on a personal basis. Even relationships in so-called small congregations can be somewhat impersonal. Therefore, a small group sponsored by a church can tie persons into the church at a more intimate level. If every member of a church has a close and personal relationship or friendship with at least six to twelve other people in the church through a small group that meets on a regular basis, that church's overall fellowship will be strong indeed. You don't need to be a close friend of every member in the church in order to feel close to that church, but only of a few. None of us has the time or energy to have close relationships with a lot of people, but we can do so in a small group, and that is enough to feel close to the church.

However, there are also some things a small group cannot do for us. A support group cannot give us "value." Others may value us, but they cannot endow us with value. The value of all persons is a given because of God's gift of value in creation. Others can make us feel important and of worth, but we have to discover our inherent value for ourselves. This can be found only in a personal relationship with God through faith in Jesus Christ.

A small group cannot make us be happy or feel good. Though others may share their own happiness and good feelings, they cannot transfer them to us. Happiness is actually a choice each one makes. Good feelings come as a by-product of doing what is right in response to the Good News of Jesus Christ.

A small group should not make your decisions for you. Your decisions must be yours, especially when related to morality, spiritual direction, economic decisions, vocational matters, or family relationships. With regard to the heavier decisions of life, we should not "pass the buck" to others to decide for us. After all, we have to live with the consequences of our decisions. We cannot and should not blame a group of friends for leading us astray if the decision proves to be a poor one. Harry had been divorced about three years and had recently decided to ask Anne to marry him. As he attended our support group one evening to test his feelings about Anne, he asked the group to assure him he would be making the right choice. Our group wisely reminded him that we could not do that. We could share our opinions about their relationship, but we could not and would not make his decision for him.

In spite of the limitations of small groups, the strengths and advantages of participation therein far outweigh possible negatives when the group is led by mature people and focuses on Jesus Christ as the Lord of the group members' lives.

Creating a Small Group

You may be asking by now, "Just how do you get a small support group started?" I am assuming that you are a Christian who is actively involved in a local church. In light of that, it has been my experience that the most effective small groups that function in the context of the church have the approval and encouragement of the pastor. Though not necessary, it would be a tremendous help if he would take the responsibility of leadership in organizing such groups. However, many pastors have neither the training nor experience in working with small groups whose focus is spiritual enlightenment and personality growth. Some are even intimidated by the idea. Others have previously had a negative experience with a small group that became critical of and even competitive with the pastor's overall leadership. But there are many innovative pastors who have read and studied the concept and are eager to run with the idea with interested lay persons.

The following are some simple suggestions that may or may not work in your particular situation. Some churches have chosen to identify their small-group ministry with an appropriate name, such as Discipleship Groups, Prayer-and-Share Groups, or simply Fellowship Groups. One church chose the Greek word for fellowship and called theirs "Koinonia" Groups. The name chosen should reflect something of the group's purpose and direction.

I have found that it helps if the pastor and a selected group of committed lay leaders and their spouses initiate a small-group experience as a beginning model for a three-or-four-month period of time. My first experiment lasted from September until just before Christmas. The group should be no larger than twelve people. The pastor and his wife might serve as conveners and leaders. Meeting once a week and rotating each session in the homes of the group, the leadership couple would model prayer, sharing, openness with regard to who we are as persons, and mutual encouragement of each other.

An immediate reaction in many churches about this would be: "Oh, no, not another meeting to attend!" There is no easy answer to this in busy churches with active members. Some groups have found the best time to be the two hours just before a Sunday-evening worship service. Others have used Wednesday evenings, with a member of the church staff leading the regular mid-week prayer meeting hour at the church and thus freeing the pastor to lead the first small-group experiment.

The sessions of the small group are loosely structured. There might be fifteen to twenty minutes spent at the beginning in expressed prayer concerns and time together in prayer, with several participating. The remainder of the two hours could be spent in sharing "who we are." This could begin in exchanging brief life-stories, including testimonies regarding conversion and subsequent Christian life. In time, this could be expanded to include "what God is doing in my life in the present" (or "what God is not doing, and possibly why"). Over a period of several weeks, such sharing eventually should focus upon the present and anticipated future. Again, the leadership couple would be the key models for this type of sharing during the early sessions. In time, the other members of the group will follow in a similar manner to share themselves.

Such a group will want to agree in advance on some guidelines:

1. To respect each other as unique persons.
2. To hold all comments in the group in confidence and not share them outside the group.
3. To have an individual "quiet time" each day involving private prayer and Bible reading.
4. To pray for each member of the group by name each day.
5. To attend each meeting of the group unless circumstantially hindered.
6. To attend the primary weekly worship service and Bible-study time of the church.
7. To determine to grow spiritually as never before.

Other commitments and disciplines may be agreed upon, but the above items will certainly be the primary ones.

At the end of the initial few months of the first group, the pastor (or other leader) may suggest that these first couples or individuals become leaders of additional new groups, with the pastor assisting in the selection of possible group members from the church rolls. By the second year, new leaders will be available from groups that met the first year, and this will expand the experience to involve more people.

Obviously, not everyone will initially want to participate in a small-group experience. However, with time and exposure a growing number of people will find the small-group experience a very meaningful and rewarding one. Such news will spread and entice others to get involved later, once the idea catches on.

Each year, primarily in September, the pastor and interested lay leaders could reconstitute new groups to keep the process going from year to year. Some problems may emerge along the way, as is true in any church activity, such as the method of selecting group members, timing and schedules, occasional personality clashes, an attitude of exclusiveness, a judgmental spirit toward the church or some aspect of its ministry, as well as the conflict of group meetings with other church activities. And some group sessions may at times seem to drag. However, since well-trained and enthusiastic leadership can avoid most of these pitfalls, the pastor will need to be responsible for training new group leaders as the number of groups increases.

The above suggestions may leave several questions unanswered for those who wish to initiate such a ministry. Therefore, additional reading and study about the idea may be needed. It will be important to start slowly and with only a few participants, to be flexible and willing to make some mistakes initially, to remain open to the leading of the Holy Spirit, and to follow your pastor's or lay leader's counsel.

If for some reason the pastor and other leaders in your church are unwilling to offer direction or encouragement, begin with sharing this book with them as you pray for the Lord's guidance and help. Prayer is often the key to initiating such new ideas in the church. Other settings offer possibilities for beginning support groups: Sunday-school class, mission-action or training groups in the church, as well as existing friendship circles of interested people.

Whatever alternate routes you may choose, do not be critical of church leaders who may not be initially interested. These are often busy people who are already overcommitted. Later they may become interested when they see the advantages and strengths of small support groups for Christian growth. Criticism may only make them defensive and uncooperative later. Working together in harmony and mutual support will more likely make any new approach succeed in time.

The Deeper Levels of Relating

After several years of working with small support groups in the context of a local church, I am thoroughly convinced that such a group offers one of the best opportunities for Christians to move into the deeper levels of interpersonal relationships and to find an amazing power for growth at those deeper levels. Now what do I mean by "deeper levels"?

In my book *We Need Each Other: Reaching Deeper Levels in Our Interpersonal Relationships* (Grand Rapids: Baker Book House, 1984), I have thoroughly discussed eight levels of relating. These are as follows:

Level One: The Avoidance Level.

Level Two: The Greeting Level.

Level Three: The Separate Interests Level.

Level Four: The Common Interests Level.

Level Five: The Social Interaction Level.

Level Six: The Caring Level.

Level Seven: The Sharing Level.

Level Eight: The Intimacy Level.

A few comments and a brief overview of these are in order here. These levels move from the shallower to the deeper, from the more distant to the closer relationships. The deeper one goes, the fewer people you relate to on each level. Notice that the first five levels are separated from the last three. This is because the three deepest levels are qualitatively different from the first five. Moving from level five to level six involves turning a very important corner.

The avoidance level includes both our unintentional and our intentional avoidance of other people. We simply do not have time to relate to most people we see each day. The greeting level is the level of recognition. Levels three and four are conversational levels and involve the search for friends. Level five is the action level, where we go beyond merely talking about interests or ideas and engage in doing them together.

A sad thing is that many people rarely if ever go beyond the fifth level with anyone. If that is the case, in time a condition I call "relational deficiency" sets in, the indicator of which is a judgmental, critical, and complaining attitude. This results because some very important ingredients are missing from one's life. Those ingredients are found on the next three levels.

Level six is the level of caring enough about others to be aware of their needs, to be present when needed, to listen, to get involved, and to reach out in specific ways of helping. The seventh level involves sharing your inner self—opening up and letting selected others know where you are "coming from" and what is happening to you—as you reveal your honest feelings and expose your "transparent self." When this occurs (and there are certainly risks involved), an exciting piece of "magic" called "reciprocity" takes place: the person you share with tends to want to share his or her life in return. Reciprocity will certainly accentuate closeness.

Level eight, the level of intimacy, is reserved for a very few people in your life, ranging from one to three. This level is very difficult to put into words and has to be experienced to be adequately understood. It is almost nonverbal in its best expression. It would take another chapter to explain it, so you might want to read my treatment of it in *We Need Each Other*.

When we reach these deeper levels, in time there develops relational sufficiency, the indicator of which is a nurturing attitude toward others. I call this the "Barnabas complex," from the man in the New Testament whose name meant Son of Encouragement (Acts 4:36). Of course, it is important to realize that we do not remain on the deeper levels all the time with everyone. Realistically speaking, we tend to move on all the levels through most days. The levels present a fluid situation, not a static one, for healthy relationships. But we all need to get to the deeper levels with some people some of the time to be relationally healthy and to keep growing.

There is a tremendous power of personality growth available on the deeper levels. The small support group, in my experience and observation, certainly can facilitate reaching the deeper levels of caring, sharing, and intimacy. My own inner vision of self did not really begin to grow until I discovered the deeper levels of relating, and I initially found these levels in a small support group of fellow believers in Christ. It was in that group that I was motivated, stimulated, and encouraged to grow, to change, and to become what I am meant to be "in Christ."

To Sum It Up

We need each other; we really do. Salvation is personal but never private. It is both individual and social. God used others to bring you and me to faith, and he wants to use others to stimulate and sustain that faith. Growth or change requires a nurturing social matrix. It rarely takes place in isolation from other believers. The new Christ-focused self-image should include involvement in Christ's body, a community of faith that offers a powerfully transforming experience in small support groups of committed and growing believers.

10

It's Okay to Love Yourself

Pauline was considered one of the "top workers" in our church. She taught a Sunday-school class, led a mission-action group of children, sang in the choir, was always present and ready to go on church visitation night, was eager to tell others about Jesus in personal evangelism efforts, and was a faithful attender at all the worship services. But she was one of the most unhappy people I have ever known. After I had been her pastor for about two years, Pauline started coming to me for personal counseling. Her initial "reason" for counseling was her "wayward son" with whom she "could do nothing." Then it was her husband who "did not understand" her and "didn't seem to care."

However, after a few sessions, the real truth came out. As we were discussing Pauline's childhood and the feelings that such a discussion brought to the surface, this middle-aged woman could hold it in no longer. She screamed out, "Oh, God, how I hate myself! I can hardly stand to look at myself in the mirror!" Then she broke into uncontrollable sobs for several minutes. Most everyone in the church considered this woman a devout Christian who loved the Lord. Yet she hated herself deeply and intensely.

Over and over again, as a pastor or an active churchman, I have been observing this major problem among professing Christians: sincere believers who do not like themselves, even hate themselves. When I have asked such people why they feel this way, they look puzzled and respond with something like, "Well, I'm a sinner and there's nothing good in me." When I suggest that maybe they need to learn to love themselves, they will even look shocked and respond, "Christians aren't supposed to love themselves. That would be pride or self-centeredness."

The blunt truth is, either directly or indirectly, these folks have been taught that they are not supposed to love themselves. They now somehow believe that spirituality requires some form of self-hate or self-rejection. Yet it is one of my deepest convictions that this is a major contradiction to basic biblical truth. Strange as it sounds, this is a highly debated subject among evangelical Christians today. In recent years, this debate has been carried on through articles in most of the leading evangelical magazines and journals.

Is Self-Love Sinful—or Good?

Is self-love something evil to be avoided—or something good to be encouraged? Some equate self-love with selfishness, self-centeredness, egotism, conceit, arrogance, and pride. Others consider self-love a divinely given moral obligation as well as a healthy approach to life and a necessary prerequisite to loving others. Which one is the biblical and Christian approach?

It is my firm belief that just as the Christian has a responsibility to others, so he or she has a basic responsibility to her or her self. However, the debate about self-love among evangelical Christians centers around the nature of the self and how it should be treated. Is the self to be loved or denied? Is it to be nurtured or condemned? Should it be liberated or mortified, affirmed or rejected? The answers to these questions depend on what we believe about salvation. What effect, if any, does God's redemptive action in Christ have upon the self of the believer? When the believer is born again (saved, redeemed, forgiven, justified, sanctified, reconciled), does any of this have a transforming effect on the self? And, to use biblical terms, which self are we talking about, the "old self" or the "new self" (cf. Eph. 4:22–24 and Col. 3:9–10)? There is a very important difference.

First we need to distinguish between "selfless love" and "self-love." These terms represent two significant viewpoints regarding the self of a believer. One view is that Christian love is purely selfless, solely an outgoing love for one's neighbor, something the Bible commands us to do. The other viewpoint states that self-love is a God-given capacity and a necessary requirement for loving others. Let us examine these ideas separately.

Selfless Love

The theory of selfless love has been carefully spelled out by many noted Christian writers over the centuries. Martin Luther (1483–1546), German monk, theologian, and leader in the Protestant Reformation, distinguished between the Roman Catholic theory of acquisitive self-love and a God-centered, self-giving love. The self is not to be loved but only given in love to and for others. Consequently, Luther's position seems to deny the validity of self-acceptance.

Leo Tolstoy (1828–1910), Russian novelist and Christian social reformer, called for an unclaiming, non-resisting, non-preferential love of neighbor, involving a preference for others over one's self. Genuine love, he said, is a present activity only; hence, future love does not exist. This is similar to what is often said today: love is something you do.

Anders Nygren, Swedish theologian (1890–1978), wrote a book some time ago titled *Agape and Eros* (New York: Harper, 1953), in which he compared divine "gift-love" with human "need-love" (to use C. S. Lewis's terms). Nygren believed that gift-love (agape) is totally incompatible with need-love (eros). Need-love is radically self-centered, greedy, and demanding. It is evil as it expresses itself in the strong desires of sensual lust; it is even more evil when it reaches out toward God to manipulate him for one's own selfish purposes. Nygren even goes so far as to say, "Christianity does not recognize self-love as a legitimate form of love." And again he says, "So far from self-love being a natural ordinance of God in nature, it is a devilish perversion." Moreover, he argues that the apostle Paul agrees: "When Paul sets self-love and neighbor-love in opposition to each other, he is not merely condemning a lower self-love . . . but all self-love whatever, even in its most highly spiritual state." Nygren's answer to man's inordinate self-love is neighbor-love. Loving neighbor "as thyself" is love turned from self to neighbor, and so the natural perversity of the will is overcome. Neighbor-love excludes and overcomes self-love, according to Nygren. However, in my judgment this sounds very much like salvation by human achievement.

Self-Love

The second theory, that of self-love, is based on the clear assumption of Jesus that it is normal and natural for you to care for, accept, and affirm yourself. When a Pharisee asked Jesus which was the greatest commandment in the Law, Jesus responded, " 'Love the Lord your God with all your heart and with all your soul and with all your mind.' This is the first and greatest commandment. And the second is like it: 'Love your neighbor as yourself' " (Matt. 22:37–38). The words "as yourself" imply an acceptance of self-love. Jesus did not say to love the neighbor "instead of yourself" but "as yourself." Notice that these words were not original with Jesus. The first commandment came from Deuteronomy 6:5 and the second from Leviticus 19:18. Therefore, love for God, neighbor, and self go back to the ancient Law of Moses given directly by God to the people of Israel. Jesus saw in these two verses the essence of "all the Law and the Prophets" (Matt. 22:40). Paul concurred with Jesus on this point (see Rom. 13:9).

Augustine, one of the Latin church fathers (354–430) and bishop of Hippo in north Africa, interpreted this self-love as loving God in ourselves since God dwells in the heart of the believer. Loving others means loving God in them. Even though Augustine implies some reservations about loving the self, it is a far improvement over self-negation or self-rejection.

The self-love theory assumes that since God so loved us in Christ, we have no right not to love that which God loves. God's love for me makes my self worth loving.

Therefore, self-love is the unconditional acceptance of one's self, created in the image of God and for whom Christ died. To flagellate the self because of its sinful nature is to sell short the death of Christ on the cross for our sins and to confuse the self with the carnal nature. Paul calls upon believers to "put to death the misdeeds of the body" (Rom. 8:13), not the self. To love, and affirm myself is to accept myself as God does, to respect myself as one created in the image of God, and to see myself as redeemed by the blood of Christ and re-created in the likeness of Jesus Christ. This does not mean that I am now perfect, sinless, and faultless. But I am worth loving: God's own example tells me so.

The biblical teachings certainly do condemn inordinate ego-tism, for this is the root of all sin (read Rom. 6 and 7). Human pride, arrogance, self-centeredness, and selfishness are expres-sions of the unregenerate self exalting itself in the face of God, rebelling against God, and even seeking to take the place of God.

Rather, I am referring here to the *new* self, the "new creation" in Christ Jesus (2 Cor. 5:17; Eph. 4:24; Col. 3:10). That new self has been "graced" by God and deserves to be loved, affirmed, ac-cepted, respected, and nurtured. This is not only good New Testa-ment theology but also good Christian psychology. Actually, Christian psychologists today are emphatically declaring that a person who chooses not to love self in a healthy acceptance and respect will have considerable difficulty loving others.

Consequently, I have cast my lot with the self-love theorists. We began with a question: Is self-love sinful—or good? If we as Chris-tians understand that we are talking about the "new self" in Christ and not the "old self" of the flesh under sin's power, that Jesus assumed the normalcy of self-love in order to express wholesome neighbor-love, and that we are not talking about self-worship or false pride, unregulated and excessive, we should have no problem understanding the value of self-love.

Moreover, there is great danger in self-negation both psycholog-ically and relationally. It could be a form of false humility. There is a biblical balance called for here: both the cross and the resur-rection are needed. These two principles, based on the historical events at the heart of the gospel of Christ, underlie the entire sixth chapter of Romans, wherein Paul calls upon us to consider our-selves as dead to sin but alive in Christ. Too many Christians put all the emphasis on dying to sin with little if any focus on being alive in Christ. Both principles are needed: ". . . count yourselves dead to sin but alive to God in Christ Jesus" (Rom. 6:11).

If at this time in your Christian life this is too heady or difficult to accept, how about beginning by letting the "Christ within" love your "self" for you and by loving the "Christ within" in return? In time he can take you the rest of the way.

The Road to Loving Yourself

A few years ago, psychiatrist M. Scott Peck wrote a best-seller entitled *The Road Less Travelled* (Simon & Schuster, 1978). The book dealt with the subject of "spiritual growth" but not from a Christian perspective as such, since that was before Peck's conversion to Christianity. But the title was intriguing and could be applied to several subjects regarding personal growth and development. It certainly applies to high self-esteem, which relates to loving yourself. The road to loving yourself, to acquiring high self-esteem, is one of those roads "less travelled."

You recall that the term *self-image* refers to the way you see yourself, your inner vision of self, what you think of yourself; while *self-esteem* refers to the way you *feel* about yourself. If you feel good about yourself, you have high self-esteem. If you feel bad or negative about yourself, you have low self-esteem.

On a popular level, Dr. Robert H. Schuller, pastor of the Garden Grove Community Church in California (which is now known as the Crystal Cathedral), has probably written and spoken nationwide on the subject of self-esteem more than anyone else. In particular, his book *Self-Esteem: the New Reformation* (Waco, Texas: Word Books, 1982) has been both praised and condemned by evangelical Christians. Even though Schuller's doctrine of sin is considered weak by the more conservative evangelicals, one of his main points is certainly valid: the church has dragged its feet in helping believers develop high self-esteem.

The church has too long tolerated what some call "worm theology," based on the words of the old hymn "At the Cross," by Isaac Watts:

> Alas! and did my Savior bleed?
> And did my Sov'reign die?
> Would He devote that sacred head
> *For such a worm as I?*

The fact of the matter is that nowhere in the Bible is a believer in Jesus Christ ever called a "worm." But Watts apparently advocated a "worm theology." Careful biblical studies in recent years are helping us to correct this.

Some readers may be asking, "But what about the Christian's sin problem?" My answer is, "The gospel, the Good News of Jesus Christ, takes care of that!" We don't need to continue wallowing in our sins of the past or present. We don't need to continue running ourselves into the ground and calling ourselves "dirt," "bad," and "good-for-nothing" because we have a sin problem. John's First Epistle was written partly to help believers deal with their sin problem. The apostle was both realistic and redemptive on this point in 1 John 1:8–9 and 2:1–2:

> If we claim to be without sin, we deceive ourselves and the truth is not in us. If we confess our sins, he is faithful and just and will forgive us our sins and purify us from all unrighteousness. . . . My dear children, I write this to you so that you will not sin. But if anybody does sin, we have one who speaks to the Father in our defense—Jesus Christ, the Righteous One. He is the atoning sacrifice for our sins. . . .

The believer's responsibility regarding his or her sin problem is confession, not self-clobbering. Christ took our clobbering for us on the cross.

So the road to loving yourself begins with the gospel. Next, as a believer in the Christ of the gospel, you need to learn to be a good "parent" to yourself. I believe this to be a very healthy approach. The Bible has a great deal to say about the fatherhood/parenthood of God. He is presented as the model for the way we should treat ourselves.

For example, God forgives: learn to forgive yourself. Pauline, mentioned at the beginning of this chapter, was a woman who for years had not forgiven herself for the sins of the past. One day in counseling we seemed to be getting nowhere on this point. So I said, "Pauline, you remind me of a person in jail who has just been pardoned or declared 'not guilty' by the court. The jailer has unlocked the door, opened it wide, and told you that you are free to go. But you won't get up and walk out a free person. You just sit there in jail, when you don't have to do so." She looked shocked. She had never thought of her situation like that. It was the beginning of her new freedom. She began to forgive herself.

Moreover, God reconciles: be reconciled to yourself. Make peace with yourself. Stop the internal battle.

In addition, God accepts you: learn to accept yourself. The concept of grace needs to be both intellectually understood and personally experienced. Learn to grace yourself as God does. Stop this morbid self-rejection.

Also, God loves you with an eternal love: learn to love yourself. You have no right to hate what God loves.

154

Finally, God affirms: learn to affirm yourself. Affirmation is one of God's marvelous characteristics. He is our heavenly Encourager. Think about it; there are many ways you can affirm yourself in all honesty. Don't be critical and judgmental of what God consistently affirms—you!

In his book *Mere Mortality* (Grand Rapids, Eerdmans, 1983), Dr. Lewis Smedes, professor of theology and ethics at Fuller Theological Seminary in California, offers five suggestions for learning to love ourselves. First, Smedes says, seeking one's own self-fulfillment is a helpful kind of self-love. God intended each of us to become what we were meant to be. A part of that intention was that we find, know, and love God, our Creator. In loving God we also love ourselves.

Second, Smedes suggests that we love ourselves well when we long for joy. The need for joy guides us to seek a feeling of being in union with the goodness of life, and knowing God is part of that goodness. Just as in knowing God we also know ourselves, to enjoy God is to enjoy ourselves. "Rejoicing in the Lord" is to feel the goodness of life. We are hypocritical if we pretend to be too selfless to seek joy for ourselves (Karl Barth).

Third, we love ourselves well when we love ourselves as members of the body of Christ, the Church. Membership in Christ's body lifts us above our aloneness. I love myself well when I have love for the body of which I am a vital member (see Eph. 5:29–30). I am not to love myself as an island but as a significant part of an even more significant whole.

Fourth, self-love can be the road to loving others. Smedes suggests, "You cannot love anyone effectively if you hate yourself. Gift-love takes a great deal of energy. We must not squander the energy we need to care for others by failing to take care of ourselves." In addition, our inner gifts must be nurtured if we are to use them for the good of others. This means that we love ourselves as a means to loving others. Such growth is a means to blessing others.

Fifth, we love ourselves well when we learn to love our spouses sexually. When a husband and wife love each other fully—with body, mind, and soul—they are also loving each's own self. Such love offers one an avenue to self-fulfillment. Paul clearly teaches this in Ephesians 5:21–31. As Smedes says, "God's agape does not eliminate eros from the treasury of his good created blessings."

Robert Schuller's book *Self-Love: The Dynamic Force of Success* (New York: Hawthorn, 1969) offers many helpful suggestions for developing a healthy self-love. The following is a summary outline of his Ten Steps:

1. Get rid of your fear of failure. We feel that failure will cause others *not* to love us. Cowardice is more shameful than failure. Understand that people accept us not so much for what we do, but for who we are.

2. Discover the unique person within you. Begin to honestly and openly share yourself with someone else, for this is a way to self-discovery. Listen with an honest ear to both "praise" and "criticism."

3. Compliment yourself. Learn to "stroke" and affirm yourself. Stop telling yourself what you're not.

4. Work to improve yourself. First, believe that you can improve or learn something. Then begin. Avoid the postponements of life—waiting until you find the "right" job or mate; until you get to be manager; until you have enough money; until the kids are through college and the mortgage is paid; until you retire; and so on.

5. Forgive yourself. Don't drag your mistakes with you. Let God's forgiveness motivate your own self-forgiveness. After all, do you know something he doesn't?

6. Accept yourself. God thinks a great deal of you; so should you. Accept your humanity and the things you cannot change.

7. Commit yourself to a great cause. Get out of the bleachers and onto the playing field. Get into something bigger than yourself. Wholesome responsibility generates self-love, for constructive responsibility fulfills the need to be needed.

8. Believe in success. God gets no joy from your desire to fail. Faith stimulates success. Hope sustains success. Love sanctifies success.

9. Strive for excellence. Do your best. Think your best. Strive to be the most thoughtful person you know.

10. Build self-love in others. Forget yourself by helping others. As they progress, you progress. Affirm both yourself and others.

As you learn to love yourself, you will discover that your self-esteem rises. You will feel good about yourself. You will enjoy yourself and, at the same time, become enjoyable to others. The ultimate hunger of the human being is the hunger for God, who is love, so getting to know God brings us into fellowship with love in its highest and deepest form. In that relationship one of the marvelous by-products is the growth of self-esteem, because God teaches us how to love ourselves. Yet remember that loving self is only a means to the end of loving others for Christ's sake. We become channels of Christ's love. Yes, it's okay to love yourself. It was God's idea in the first place.

Unconditional Love: God's Love

When we say it's okay to love yourself, exactly what kind of love are we talking about? "Gift-love" or "need-love"? It seems to me that somehow both are involved in God's design for his people. For Nygren the two kinds of love are incompatible. Yet for those who are "new creations" in Christ, it seems that Nygren was wrong, since gift-love does not force us to turn against our need-loves, any more than Christ calls us to choose between God's salvation and God's creation. As Smedes comments in *Mere Mortality:* "Rather than rejecting eros as an enemy, agape redeems eros and sets it free to be a friend." He continues: "If we believe that eros can be a friend to Christian love, we also affirm our love for ourselves. Jesus neither condemns nor praises self-love, but his saying that we should love others as we love ourselves leads us to suppose that self-love can be as good as it is natural."

It seems to me that Christians should love themselves as God loves his children: unconditionally yet redemptively. God loves us just the way we are, warts and all. He lays down no prior conditions, such as "I love you if you are good, clean, moral, religious, kind, and so on." God simply says, "I love you, regardless of what you have done or what you are like." Paul put it like this: "But God demonstrates his own love for us in this: While we were still sinners, Christ died for us" (Rom. 5:8).

God's love is not only unconditional, but it is also a sacrificial-giving love. "Christ died for us," Paul announced as the proof of God's love. John agreed: "This is love: not that we loved God, but that he loved us and sent his Son as an atoning sacrifice for our sins" (1 John 4:10). To love oneself with sacrificial-giving love means to pay whatever price is necessary to meet one's highest needs, which are primarily spiritual. This is most likely what Paul meant when he wrote: "I have been crucified with Christ and I no longer live, but Christ lives in me. The life I live in the body, I live by faith in the Son of God, who loved me and gave himself for me" (Gal. 2:20).

It is interesting that when Paul said, ". . . and I no longer live," he used the emphatic Greek term *ego* for "I." This is the word for "self." The Greek word comes directly into English as "ego," meaning the self. Therefore, for Paul the old self is crucified with Christ so that Christ can now live within the believer's life. This is the new self we are to love, the Christ being "formed" (Gal. 4:19) in us. That is the redemptive dimension.

Loving one's self "in Christ" is also accepting one's humanity. Having been made in the image of God and re-created in Christ, we should accept ourselves as human beings, including all our limitations, shortcomings, and faults. We are not perfect, only in process.

This means we are to love what is not perfect. God loves the imperfect; so should we. Isn't this the way you love your friends? You do not demand perfection from them. Self-love is being a good friend to yourself.

I have discovered that there is great power in unconditional love. I am referring to the power to change, to grow, to move forward toward God's ultimate goal for your life. Unconditional love is one of the greatest motivators to growth that I know of. I am reminded here of the incomparable way Robert Schuller tells the story of Don Quixote as a parable of the transforming power of unconditional love. We can easily apply the story to ourselves. I quote directly:

> Don Quixote, the Man of La Mancha, beautifully illustrates the gospel of Jesus Christ. Cervantes portrayed the Ideal One as Don Quixote. Any Ideal One is going to be called crazy by the world; and they called the Man of La Mancha crazy. So he asked, "Who's crazy? Am I crazy because I can see the world as it could become? Or are you crazy because you see the world as it is? Who's really crazy?"
>
> I have thought about that question, and I believe the Man of La Mancha is right. I'm not crazy if I'm an idealist. I'm not crazy if I'm a beautiful dreamer. People are crazy who only see the world as it is. They're crazy because they're not creative; they're crazy because they are not uplifting sources. Because they're not part of the solution, they keep the world as it is.

"I am not what I think I am; I am not what you think I am; I am what I think you think I am." If you say we are all sinners, you're right. I agree with you. Your condemnations only reinforce my own rebellion. So don't tell me what I am—tell me what I might become.

The Man of La Mancha sees this harlot, this whore, this Mary Magdalene. Aldonza is her name. She's a waitress by day and a prostitute by night. She serves the drunken camel drivers. The Man of La Mancha says to this whore, "My Lady." She looks at him and exclaims, "Lady?" Some camel driver makes a pass at her and she squeals . . . . laughs. The Man of La Mancha says, "Yes, you are My Lady, and I shall give you a new name. I shall call you Dulcinea. You are My Lady . . . . you are my Lady, Dulcinea."

Once, in distress, not comprehending him, when they are alone, she says, "Why do you do and say these things? Why do you treat me the way you do? What do you want from me? I know men. I've seen them all; I've had them all; they're all the same. They all want something from me. Why do you say these things? Why do you call me Dulcinea? Why do you call me your Lady? What do you want?" He says, "I just want to call you what you are . . . . you are My Lady, Dulcinea."

Later there is a horrible scene backstage. You hear screams . . . . she is being raped. She runs onto the stage. She has been insulted with the ultimate indignity and she's crying and hysterical, dirty and disheveled. Her blouse has been torn off and her skirt is ripped. He sees her and says compassionately, "My Lady, Dulcinea, Oh, My Lady, My Lady."

She can't stand it and cries, "Don't call me a Lady. Oh God, don't call me a Lady. Can't you see me for what I am? I was born in a ditch by a mother who left me there naked and cold—too hungry to cry. I never blamed her. She left me there hoping I'd have the good sense to die. Don't call me a Lady. I'm only a kitchen slut, reeking with sweat. I'm only a whore men use and forget. Don't call me your Lady. I'm only Aldonza. I am nothing at all."

As she runs into the night of self-flagellation, he calls out, "But you *are* My Lady." The curtain drops.

The curtain rises again. The Man of La Mancha is dying, like our Lord, from a broken heart, despised and rejected of men, a man of sorrows and acquainted with grief. To his deathbed comes a Spanish queen with a mantilla of lace. She kneels, makes the sign of the cross, and prays. He opens his eyes and says, "Who are you?" She replies, "My Lord, don't you remember? You sang a song, don't you remember? 'To dream the impossible dream, to fight the unbeatable foe, to bear the unbearable sorrow, to run where the brave dare not go . . .' My Lord, don't you remember? You gave me a new name, you called me Dulcinea." She stands proudly. "I am your Lady." And the angels sing, and he goes to be with his Father. It is finished. She was born again. [From Robert H. Schuller, "Pastoring and Evangelizing for Self-Esteem," *Your Better Self: Christianity, Psychology, and Self-Esteem*, Craig W. Ellison, Editor, San Francisco: Harper & Row, 1983, pp. 199–201.]

This is the way God relates to us in Christ, and I believe that we should treat ourselves in the same way. It's okay to love yourself— your *new* self in Christ.

To Sum It Up

It is a tragedy for Christians not to love themselves. It is a greater tragedy for Christians to despise or hate themselves. If you have been taught that it is not okay for you to love yourself, you have been taught something that is not in the Bible. Self-hate is not a mark of spirituality; rather, it is a sign of spiritual sickness. We too often hear it said that "the preacher really preached a great sermon: he stepped all over our toes." But if people go to church to get sermonically whipped in order to feel good, they need to re-examine the Bible. Such an attitude is spiritual masochism. It is sick religion.

With "Christ in you," what do you see? Does such an inner vision call for rejection or for love?

God is no heavenly sadist. He wants you to feel good about yourself as one of his children. "In Christ" you have been given every reason to have the highest self-esteem.

I agree with Lewis Smedes when he writes in *Mere Mortality*: "God's gift-love which came in Jesus was meant not to destroy but to liberate his creation. It is not love of self, but love of self alone, which is sinful. Indeed we ought to love ourselves so that we can be loving agents of God's love."

11

Seeing Determines Doing

Why is your inner vision of self so important? Because it determines how you behave. What you see is what you do. Self-vision is a process of selecting and wearing a cluster of labels that define and describe what kind of person you see yourself to be. The inner mirror of your self-image portrays you wearing a variety of personality labels. These labels are very powerful, for they describe what you see when you look at yourself.

Proving the Labels Are True

As we have seen, the power of the labels comes largely from an inner compulsion to prove that the labels are true. Proving the labels are true is your psyche's way of maintaining its "sanity," or emotional balance. Whether the labels are true to the facts is not perceived to be important. What is important is that you prove that your inner vision is "true" by behaving in accord with what the labels describe.

When Jake Parsons was referred to me for counseling by his attorney, the immediate problem was that Jake's live-in girlfriend

161

had recently kicked him out of her apartment. Jake was emotionally distraught, at times crying uncontrollably. "She's been the only person who ever loved me," he cried out through his tears. In a few minutes, I learned that Jake, now thirty-four years old, had spent six years in prison on three separate occasions since he was nineteen. His parents were almost totally irresponsible people, having had thirteen children, of whom only nine were still living. Most of them had been raised by other relatives. Jake was raised by his "very strict" maternal grandparents. He had never been close to any of his brothers and sisters. He said he really did not know his father, whom he had seen only twice in the last ten years. His parents had divorced years ago, and his mother, now fifty-two, had been married three times since then. In recent years she has had nothing to do with Jake.

Jake's only early memory before age six was one day at age four when his father held him up by his arm and severely cut him across his legs with his belt several times. Jake said his legs were "a bleeding mess" when his father finally dropped him on the floor. While being beaten he thought his arm would twist off at the shoulder. This horrible experience was forever etched on his mind and fueled occasional rage toward all those who were supposed to love him.

Jake's girlfriend kicked him out after two years of brutal physical and emotional abuse by this emotionally unstable man. Three labels could clearly be identified in Jake's inner vision of himself: "rejected," "loser," and "angry." And his behavior was proving that every one of them was true. Jake was a high-school dropout ("My teachers told me I was stupid"), had never learned a trade or skill by which to make a decent living ("I can only pick up odd jobs"), had already been married and divorced once ("My wife really never loved me"), had gone to prison, each time for stealing ("I knew I would get caught"), was presently unemployed ("Nobody wants to hire me"), and had no personal friends ("Nobody likes me").

I sought to lead Jake to faith in Christ, but his response was: "That's too good to be true; it would never work for me." After a couple of counseling sessions, I never saw him again. He failed to show up for his third appointment. I was able to get his ex-girlfriend in touch with a local church that was able in time to

reach her for conversion and church membership. She needed
spiritual help as much as Jake did. She was almost as emotionally
"sick" as he was, having tolerated his abuse for so many months.
This was a classic case of "love" between a sadist and a masochist! But the masochist was finally getting tired of the beatings.

Pauline, mentioned in the last chapter, was equally trapped in a
cluster of negative labels. Yet she was an active professing Christian who had "all the spiritual answers" for her non-Christian ac-
quaintances and neighbors. It wasn't until she changed her
self-image that her behavior began to change. When she adopted
new biblical labels for her Christian identity, she began to prove
they were true by a new quality of action.

As with all human behavior, Christian behavior is goal-
oriented. The new biblical labels become the new goals toward
which we strive. The labels are our perception and become the
goals of our behavior. Therefore, perception—inner vision, self-
image, what you see in yourself, what you think of yourself—is a
powerful determiner of action. Seeing determines doing.

The Christian with a Negative Self-image

There are a lot of "Paulines" in the church today. They sincerely
want to worship and serve God through Jesus Christ. These people are a lot like the apostle Paul before his Damascus Road experience with the risen Jesus (cf. Acts 9 and Rom. 7 and 8): driven,
determined, uptight, angry, frustrated, miserable, and convinced
that they are "right." But deep inside they know something is
missing. By this I do not mean that all unhappy church members
with negative self-images are unsaved. They simply have not come
all the way past the Easter event. Or, as it is sometimes said, "They
have been to the cross but not to the resurrection." I do not mean
to sound overly pietistic or devotional at this point. I am simply
saying they have not heard all of the gospel.

If you, as a professing Christian, have non-Christian presuppo-
sitions that have never been challenged (e.g., "even in Christ I am
still unloved, unwanted, a no-good or stupid person"), and you
continue to see life or the world as a horrible place from which
you need to escape, and you spend more time feeling insecure,
critical, and angry than you do feeling loved, secure, free, valued,

and at peace, then you simply have not heard all of the gospel of Christ. Your faith is somewhat half-baked and your new birth is probably premature. You may be a spiritual "preemie."

Moreover, the Christian with a negative self-image will experience a great deal of inner frustration and unhappiness. The Reverend Wallace Dawson is a bi-vocational pastor who supplements his small church salary with a variety of jobs on the side. His wife, Janis, teaches school and most of the time earns more money than does her husband. Wallace and Janis came to me initially for marriage counseling with considerable conflict in their marital relationship. Wallace had a strange mix of contradictory elements in his personality but began his call to ministry with much promise. He was already in his thirties and had a family when he began his college work. Upon graduation he attended a graduate theological seminary. Yet, for the past ten years or so, with both a bachelor's and a master's degree in hand, his life was one failure after another. He had been pastor of two churches, having been fired by the first one, and the second assignment was exceptionally small, with fewer than fifteen in attendance on Sundays.

Wallace's income was minimal, and Janis had become extremely angry over the fact that her husband was doing so little to improve their economic plight. Moreover, Wallace believed that the husband was to be the literal "head" (meaning "boss" to him) of the home, telling everyone what to do. Their three sons especially resented their father's dictatorial attitude, when in reality their mother was buying the groceries and paying the rent with her income. In more ways than not the relationships in the family were rather stressful.

Personality-inventory tests revealed that Wallace was plagued with a deeply rooted inferiority complex. His poor self-image centered around a perception of "unwanted" and "unloved." Moreover, he saw himself in relationships as a "loser." Yet every Sunday Wallace preached two sermons on the Good News of Jesus Christ. His messages pointed in one direction while his inner vision of himself pointed in another. Here was a Christian (and a preacher at that) who had a very negative self-image and was filled with considerable frustration and unhappiness. His poor self-image had almost wrecked his career as well as his marriage before he was fifty years old.

In addition, Christians with a negative self-image will feel an inner compulsion to misbehave. By "misbehave" I mean they will, on a regular basis, either violate their moral values or create considerable conflict in their interpersonal relationships. In Wallace's case he was choosing to precipitate conflict in the family: he was harsh with his sons and overbearing with his wife. He knew nothing about tender listening and understanding of their needs. He demanded that his boys "do their chores around the house" and that his wife "clean house, cook the meals, and give him lots of sexual pleasure." Yet *he* was the major problem in the home. He saw to it that the family was constantly in some kind of conflict over his expectations.

In recent years the media world has played upon the shock value of publicizing the misbehavior of a few television evangelists: unethical methods in fund raising, sexual indiscretions, volatile attacks on each other in the electronic church, and the questionable use of funds for personal gain, involving conspicuous and luxurious consumption far beyond reason. To my knowledge, no in-depth psychological study of these TV preachers has been made, but from what I have read and observed about them, it is my strong suspicion that some of these people are plagued with the negative V.I.P. syndrome that often includes a built-in self-destruct mechanism. One would hope that these men are not typical. Certainly the advances of modern technology have facilitated the spread of the Good News. Unfortunately, a few rotten apples have caused Christians and non-Christians alike to lose confidence in the motives of popular televangelists, if not in their message.

The Christian with a negative self-image will in some way rationalize his or her misbehavior. Wallace was good at this. Nothing was ever his fault. Conflict, he claimed, existed because no one in the family "respected" him. He was the good daddy and the loving husband. What else could they want from him? Any exposure of his weaknesses met with stern resistance. The problem was not with him; it was with "those disrespectful boys" and his "distant, unappreciative wife."

In like fashion, misbehaving media ministers are also good at explaining away their unethical and un-Christian actions. One who was involved in a very nasty scandal in which he openly admitted his complicity claimed that he was the target of vicious attacks and attempts to take over his multimillion-dollar ministry.

By making the other fellows look much worse, he rationalized that his sins were much less serious than theirs.

Finally, since Christians with a negative self-image will ultimately put themselves down, they will unknowingly put down what the gospel represents. Although Wallace would defend himself as "right," he eventually began punishing himself with a sort of merciless self-torture. When he would describe his childhood, it was always a "pity trip" of the most severe type. His parents did not really love him, while his brothers and a sister tended to ignore him, or so he said. Wallace admitted in counseling that he had always had to struggle with a deep feeling of inferiority. I once asked him if he believed himself to be inferior. After several minutes of contemplative silence, he responded, "Yes, I guess I must be, and everyone else in my life thinks so." He then showed me his college and seminary transcripts; his grades averaged a low *C.* Yet he was a very studious person.

I once asked Wallace how he reconciled his harsh self-criticisms and personality put-downs with the Good News he preached on Sundays. He had never thought about that; it was a totally new idea. For the first time in his ministry, he saw the contradiction between how he saw and treated himself and what he preached to his congregation. Here was a gospel preacher who had not really heard all the gospel himself!

If Jesus Christ has given you a "new self" that is positive and affirmed by God, how can you continue to cling tenaciously to an old, stale, and negative self-image? Hear the whole gospel: "Therefore, if anyone is in Christ, he is a new creation; the old has gone, the new has come! (2 Cor. 5:17).

The Christian with a Positive Self-image

One of the primary objectives of this book has been to guide the Christian toward the development of a positive self-image, which in turn will produce Christ-like behavior. Earlier I said that the power of one's personality labels comes largely from an inner compulsion to prove that the labels are true. When you become a Christian, the Holy Spirit desires to replace your old labels (describing your "old self") with new labels (describing your "new self") and to shepherd your inner compulsion to prove the labels are true with Christ-like behavior.

The new labels define the goals toward which the Spirit guides all believers. Since these new goals describe or portray the nature and character of God in Jesus Christ, we can conclude that the Christian with a positive Christ-centered self-image *has* heard the whole gospel. Such a one has gone past a mere decision-oriented faith to the process of growth in Christ-like character.

I have also argued in this book that the Christian with a positive self-image has taken on a new set of labels that are clearly set forth in the Scriptures. In some cases I have used more contemporary terms to interpret what the biblical materials say about the labels of the "new self" in Christ. I have identified the following: loved, valued, responsible, capable, free, secure, attractive, cooperative, nurturer, happy, and realistic. These become the new goals toward which the Christian strives in the power of the Holy Spirit. Moreover, the Christian with a positive self-image is daily reinforcing those new labels through Bible study and prayer. Such reinforcement offers the believer a tremendous motivation to maintain a meaningful devotional life.

As a Christian, I am in the process of asking and answering three questions on a daily basis: (1) Who am I? (2) What am I? (3) What am I to be and do? Answering those questions presents a lifetime challenge. One never gets too old or experienced to believe that those questions have been forever and thoroughly answered. The content of the Bible, when properly read and interpreted, can function to help me answer those questions.

"Who am I?" causes me to reflect upon my basic identity. What are my spiritual roots? How did I get here? From where? From whom? Only at my physical birth and from my parents? For the Christian, it seems to me that the question in time is transformed into "*Whose* am I?" My identity flows out of my Creator's plan for redemption, which is worked through my commitment to Jesus Christ and being possessed by him. The Scriptures often address my spiritual identity, and I need a daily reinforcement of that identity.

The question "What am I?" addresses what kind of person I am as a follower of Jesus Christ. The answer will focus upon the basic character of the believer. This comes very close to what we mean by self-image. What kind of person do you see when you look at yourself? The Scriptures also speak to the subject of the kind of person the child of God is called to be. For example, the Bible describes the follower of Jesus as a forgiving person. We all know from experience that there are times when that is "humanly" impossible. Most of us could say in all honesty, "I am not naturally a forgiving person, especially when I have been greatly offended." But the Bible describes those in the kingdom of God as both forgiven and forgiving. Therefore, I need a daily reinforcing of that description of what I am as a newborn person in Jesus Christ.

The answer to the third question, "What am I to be and do?" depends on how I answered the first two, since it represents a logical summary of character and action. Who I am and what I am set the agenda for what I am to *do*. The Bible has much to say about this also. Paul's "therefore's" (e.g., Rom. 12:1; 14:13, 19; 1 Cor. 15:58; 2 Cor. 4:1; Gal. 4:31; Eph. 2:11; 6:13; Phil. 2:12; 4:1; Col. 3:5; 1 Thess. 5:11) lead into Christian action based upon God's redemptive work in shaping the believer's character. On the basis of what God has done for us in Christ, here is what we are expected to do. This is Paul's style of setting forth guidelines for the Christian life. And I need a daily reinforcement of understanding these guidelines. The Christian with a positive self-image has established a new set of behavioral goals. As the biblical labels that describe one's new Christian identity become slowly reinforced, these labels provide specific goals for one's growth in the Christian life.

For example, when I first began counseling Pauline, I found her to be a very insecure person. She had been reared in an atmosphere of conditional love. As a child, her father had very little to do with her, and her mother loved her with a moralistic tone of "I love you if . . . ." Pauline never really felt loved, since she never measured up to all of mother's expectations. She was never quite good enough. This conditional love left her with a lot of inner insecurity.

In time, the counseling process guided Pauline to cast off her old "insecure" label and clothe herself with a new one that read "secure." Several weeks of studying the biblical passages on fear and worry gave her scriptural reinforcement for her growing sense of inner security. She gave special attention to Jesus' teaching about anxiety vs. trust (Matt. 6:25–34; Luke 12:22–31) as well as the many references to "fear not" throughout the Bible. In addition, a study of the biblical teachings on prayer reinforced her newly born confidence in the providence of God. Over a period of several months, I watched this woman become serenely secure, emotionally stable, patient with life, and tolerant of others. She learned how to grow toward the goal of security as she began seeing herself inwardly as "secure" in Christ. This is but one example of how new labels call forth new goals and changed behavior.

Obviously, the Christian with a positive self-image will in time experience enhanced self-esteem. Without a doubt, I can testify that as my self-image has improved by means of the biblical relabeling process, I have gradually begun to feel good about myself. And why not? Every description of the child of God in the Bible is a positive, affirming one. At the highest level of biblical revelation, there is no "worm theology." God's people have every possible reason to feel positive about themselves.

Somewhere in my reading of British history, I came across a story from the childhood life of Edward VII (1841–1910), who—as heir to the throne of England—was titled "Prince of Wales." One day at Windsor Castle five-year-old Edward was playing on the castle grounds with his nanny. After a while she decided to go back into the castle for a sweater. In those few minutes alone, a bored Edward saw his chance to dash outside the castle walls into the surrounding village streets hoping to find some playmates his age.

Not far into the village of Windsor, Edward came upon a park where a group of village waifs was playing. These little boys, about Edward's age, bore the outward signs of the lowest levels of poverty: dirty, grubby, ragged clothes; disheveled hair; and unwashed bodies. They had no idea who Edward was. It did not matter that he was clean and neatly dressed, since children that age tend not to pay much attention to society's externals. So Edward simply joined in to play with these new friends.

Before long a policeman walked by and chided the children, "Boys, boys, can't you read the sign? You're not supposed to play on the grass here in the park!" But little Edward simply stood up and said to the bobby, "We'll play here if we wish!" "Oh, you will, will you? And just who do you think you are?" Without a moment's hesitation, Edward calmly replied, with head held high and shoulders back, "Sir, I am the Prince of Wales."

Standing next to Edward was a little boy whose clothes were tattered and torn, whose body smelled like he hadn't had a bath in over a month, who was as dirty and grubby as a child of poverty could be. He thought Edward was pulling a good one on the policeman. He had no idea who Edward was, but he liked the new boy's spunk so much he responded, "Yeah, that's right, he's the Prince of Wales, so get lost!"

Being somewhat stunned and taken back with such childish arrogance, the policeman turned to this ragamuffin and asked, "And just who do you think *you* are?" The little fellow, having been inspired by Edward's example, stood up straight and tall, with chest out, shoulders back, and head held high, replied, "Sir, I am the Archbishop of Canterbury!"

A new identity, a new inspiration, a new example of a positive self-image, and a daring spirit gave this pitiful little person from the pits of poverty a new sense of self-esteem. Is it any different with the Christian who has been snatched from the jaws of sin's slavery? Formerly condemned, lost, blind, enslaved, polluted, stained, and marked for eternal death, the sinner saved by God's grace and redeemed by the blood of Christ acquires a new identity.

When Jesus confronted Satan on the Mount of Temptation (Matt. 4:1–11), the devil sought to deter Jesus from his life's purpose to be the Savior of the world. In a sense, Satan was asking Jesus, "Just who do you think you are?" And Jesus was responding in each temptation experience, "I am the Son of God!" Likewise, when you and I confess faith in Jesus Christ, we are like that little ragamuffin at Windsor, as we concur, "Yeah, that's right. He's the Son of God!" But watch out! For the rest of our life, Satan will turn to us thousands of times and ask, "Well, just who do you think *you* are?" The Bible implies we can stand tall and straight, with chest out, shoulders back, and head held high, and respond, "I am a child of the King!" No personal put-downs, no groveling in the dust, no self-image negations: the disciple of Christ is a child of the King, an heir to heaven's glory. The highest self-esteem can be yours.

Finally, the Christian with a positive self-image will become a person who nurtures others to follow. Those of us who have had a difficult time moving from a negative to a positive self-image, but have now discovered the freedom and joys of high self-esteem, feel an inner compulsion to share the Good News and thereby encourage those who still struggle with low self-esteem to "cross the Jordan into the Promised Land." This book is a product of my own struggles and subsequent victory, which I have wanted to share with a wider audience than the limited number of people who have been coming to me for counseling. My counseling strategy has been one of probing into the heart of the counselee's self-image and nurturing the person toward changing his or her negative labels.

One of the labels identified in the positive self-image is that of "nurturer." Such an inner vision motivates one to be giving, expressive, and demonstrative. In one church where I was the pastor, one of our members was Gene Little, a young man who had a marvelously positive self-image. Gene's job required him to work with large wattages of electricity, and his personality was certainly "electrifying" wherever he went. In our church he was known as a "hugger" and "the happy one," and his positive exuberance was inspiring to others. His joy rubbed off because Gene openly shared the source of his joy—his relationship with Jesus Christ. More than that, he encouraged those with a poor self-image to find in Christ a new vision of themselves. I have never known anyone quite like him.

Perception of Christ Produces Imitation of Christ

My basic thesis (What you see is what you do) could be interpreted and applied from a very secular or humanistic viewpoint. But my theology will not allow me to do that, even if I wanted to do so. I have suggested that your best possible inner vision of self must come from a clear perception of Jesus Christ rather than from some other criterion. This perception needs to begin with the witness of the gospel, the Good News of Christ, followed by a personal experience with Christ himself, which includes the forgiveness of sin and reconciliation with God. Then comes a continuing process of growth in which the Holy Spirit shapes the new self with biblical truth, the source of the new labels for one's personality.

First the *Word* of Christ declares your new identity. You find in the biblical witness the nature and character of who you are in Christ. This is to state again the absolutely essential role of the Bible in the believer's life, with emphasis on daily exposure thereto.

Then the *Spirit* of Christ enables your new behavior. Merely knowing the ultimate objective of the Christian life is not enough. The pattern requires the power. The process of growing in Christ is not a human achievement; it is a divine enablement. Salvation is a process whereby God shapes a new person. Changed behavior, from a Christian perspective, comes about because God makes it possible. Paul reminds us that "he who began a good work [salvation] in you will carry it on to completion until the day of Christ Jesus" (Phil. 1:6).

Finally, the *Body* of Christ demonstrates your new humanity. The transformation of your self-image is never to be seen as some limited form of individual alteration of one's personality. The quality of change brought about by Jesus Christ is always bigger than the individual. It includes a corporate, social, group experience. What happens to us as individual believers always involves the people of God, the family of faith—the body of Christ, the church. We are not isolated recipients of divine blessings. We are a "chosen people, a royal priesthood, a holy nation, a people belonging to God" (1 Pet. 2:9). This new humanity has been reconciled to God by the cross of Christ and gathered from diverse and fragmented parts into a single household (Eph. 2:14–22). What Jesus Christ designs to do in our individual lives, he brings together in his body, which collectively demonstrates the new humanity. The most positive and affirming group of people in all the world should be the church of Jesus Christ.

To Sum It Up

Perception is the key to action. Tell me what you see in yourself, and I'll tell you what you do. Seeing determines doing. Christians with a negative self-image and low self-esteem have not come all the way into the center of the gospel. The Good News calls each of us to see ourselves "in Christ," and to clothe ourselves with the new identity that is ours in him.

Theologians of an earlier generation often wrote about the "vision of God." The prophet Isaiah had such a vision of God that he was driven to despair until the vision brought forgiveness and reconciliation. Then he found himself a new person with a new set of goals for his life, given to him by God himself (Isa. 6:1–9).

Moses had a vision of God (Exod. 33—34) that transformed his

entire understanding of life. On one occasion, the apostle Paul reflected upon this vision and concluded that in Jesus Christ we
have a better and clearer vision than Moses had. Moses had only a
partial and temporary understanding of God's will for his people.
But in Jesus Christ the full and final insight into the nature, character, and will of God is made known (John 1:17–18). Paul summa-
rizes this concept: "And we, who with unveiled faces all reflect the
Lord's glory, are being transformed into his likeness with ever-
increasing glory, which comes from the Lord, who is the Spirit"
(2 Cor. 3:18).

The "vision of God" in Jesus Christ is seen supremely and most
clearly in the cross and resurrection of Jesus. Such a vision
should be at the heart of our worship in the church. From such
worship flows the inevitable willingness to serve: "Here am I.
Send me!" (Isa. 6:8). "In Christ" we can then respond to Paul's ex-
hortation in Romans 12:1–2:

> Therefore, I urge you, brothers, in view of God's mercy, to offer
> your bodies as living sacrifices, holy and pleasing to God—this is
> your spiritual act of worship. Do not conform any longer to the pat-
> tern of this world, but be transformed by the renewing of your
> mind. Then you will be able to test and approve what God's will is—
> his good, pleasing and perfect will.

Seeing determines doing. What you see is what you do. Christian visionetics and self-affirmation offer you a new way of seeing
yourself and therefore a new way to live. The power of the positive
self-image "in Christ" is truly "the power of God unto salvation."

For Further Reading

These titles represent a mixture of viewpoints regarding the self-image, both religious and secular. Not everything in these books is in harmony with the theological perspective of my own views set forth in this book. However, these authors have been stimulating to my thinking and may prove helpful to you as well, if you read with biblical discrimination. Light from the social sciences is as much "light" as is light from the Bible, theology, and the experience and observations of pastoral ministry. However, God is the Author of all truth and, in the hierarchy of truth sources, the Bible is our supreme source. It therefore should provide the test of the validity of all other sources.

Burwick, Ray. *Self-Esteem: You're Better Than You Think*. Wheaton, Ill.: Tyndale, 1983.

Dodson, Fitzhugh. *The You That Could Be*. New York: Pocket Books, 1977.

Ellison, Craig W., ed. *Your Better Self: Christianity, Psychology and Self-Esteem*. San Francisco: Harper & Row, 1983.

Kinzer, Mark. *The Self-Image of a Christian: Humility and Self-Esteem*. Ann Arbor, Mich.: Servant Books, 1980.

Lair, Jess. *"Ain't I a Wonder . . . and Ain't You a Wonder Too!" Winning Freedom Through Acceptance.* Garden City, N.Y.: Doubleday, 1977.

McGinnis, Alan Loy. *Bringing Out the Best in People.* Minneapolis: Augsburg, 1985.

Maltz, Maxwell, M.D. *The Magic Power of Self-Image Psychology.* New York: Pocket Books, 1970.

Missildine, W. Hugh, M.D. *Your Inner Child of the Past.* New York: Pocket Books, 1963.

Osborne, Cecil. *The Art of Understanding Yourself.* Grand Rapids: Zondervan, 1967.

_____. *The Art of Learning to Love Yourself.* Grand Rapids: Zondervan, 1976.

Peck, M. Scott, M.D. *The Road Less Travelled.* New York: Simon & Schuster, 1978.

Rubin, Theodore Isaac, M.D. *Compassion and Self-Hate: An Alternative to Despair.* New York: Ballantine Books, 1975.

Satir, Virginia. *Peoplemaking.* Palo Alto, Calif.: Science & Behavior Books, 1972.

Schuller, Robert H. *Self-Love: The Dynamic Force of Success.* New York: Hawthorne Books, 1969.

_____. *Self-Esteem: The New Reformation.* Waco, Tex.: Word Books, 1982.

Thornton, Edward E. *Being Transformed: An Inner Way of Spiritual Growth.* Philadelphia: Westminster Press, 1984.

Ward, Ruth. *Self-Esteem: A Gift from God.* Grand Rapids: Baker Book House, 1986.

Wilson, Earl D. *The Discovered Self: The Search for Self-Acceptance.* Downers Grove, Ill.: InterVarsity Press, 1985.

Wright, H. Norman. *Improving Your Self Image.* Eugene, Oreg.: Harvest House, 1983.